Magic Mandala Coloring Book

Copyright: Published in the United States by Karen Sanderson
Published January 2017
ISBN-13: 978-1542679732
ISBN-10: 1542679737

All rights reserved. No part of this publication may be reproduced, stored in retrieval system, copied in any form or by any means, electronic, mechanical, photocopying, recording or otherwise transmitted without written permission from the publisher. Please do not participate in or encourage piracy of this material in any way. You must not circulate this book in any format. Karen Sanderson *does not control or direct users' actions and is not responsible for the information or content shared, harm and/or actions of the book readers.*

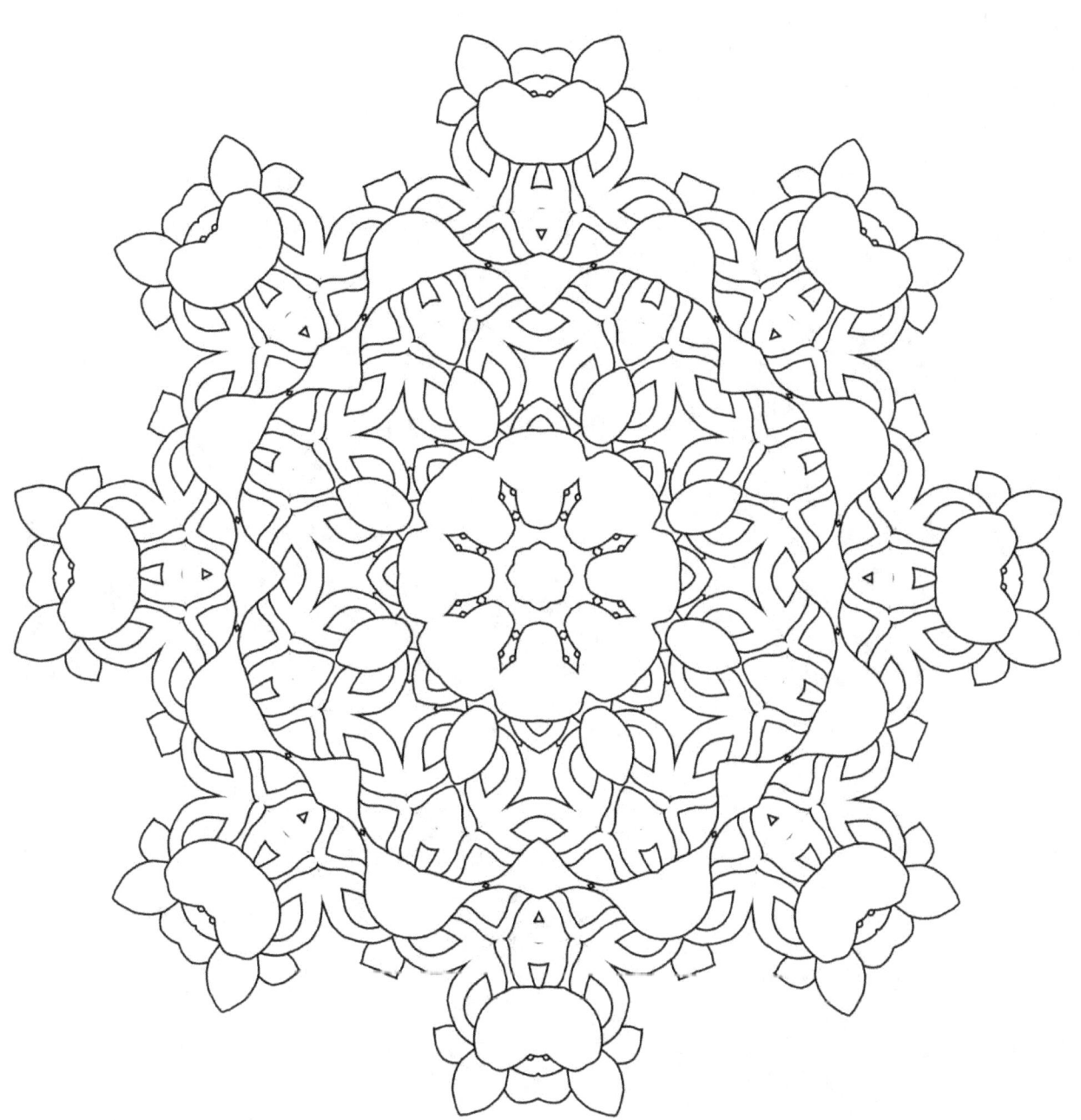

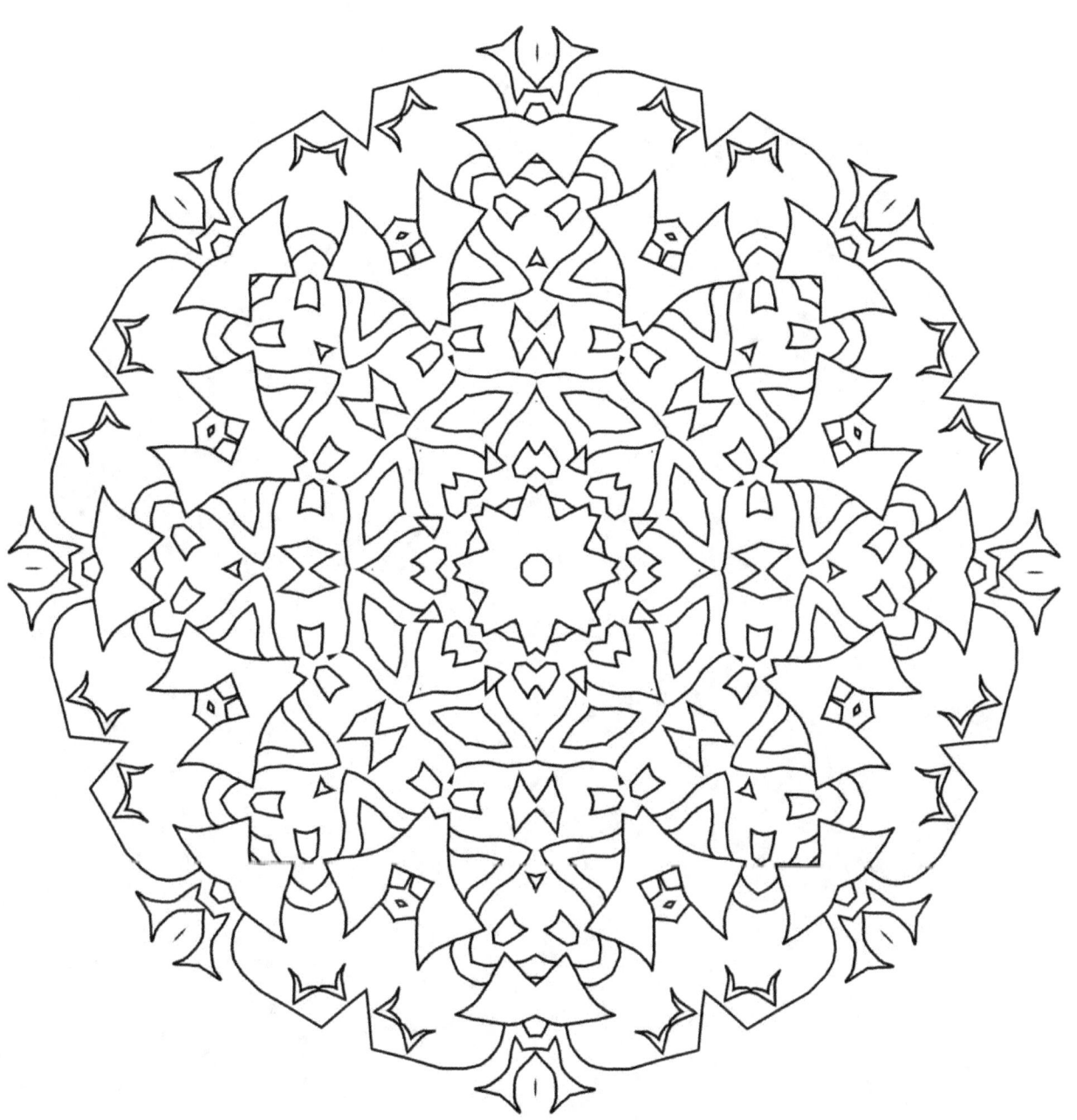

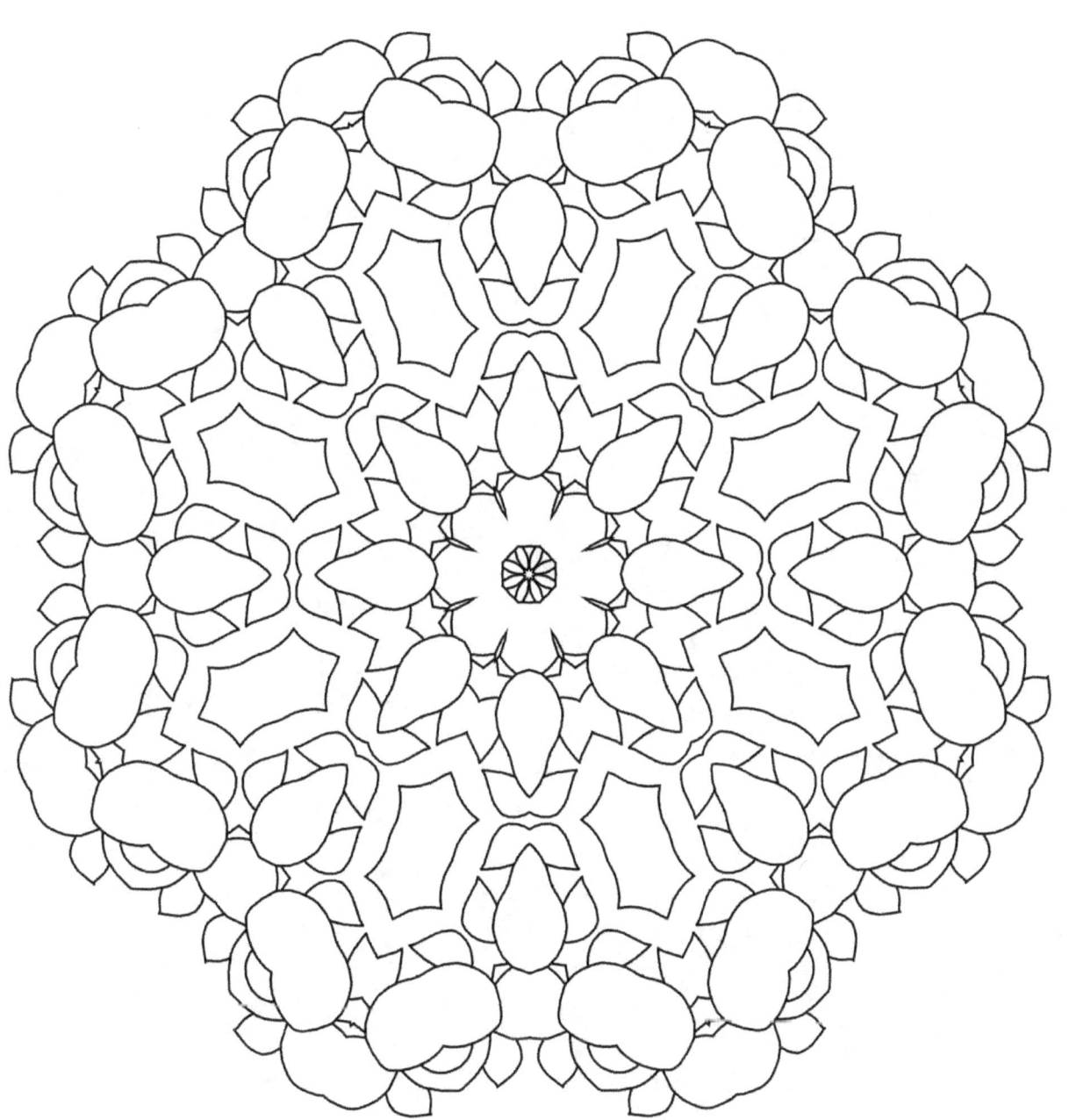

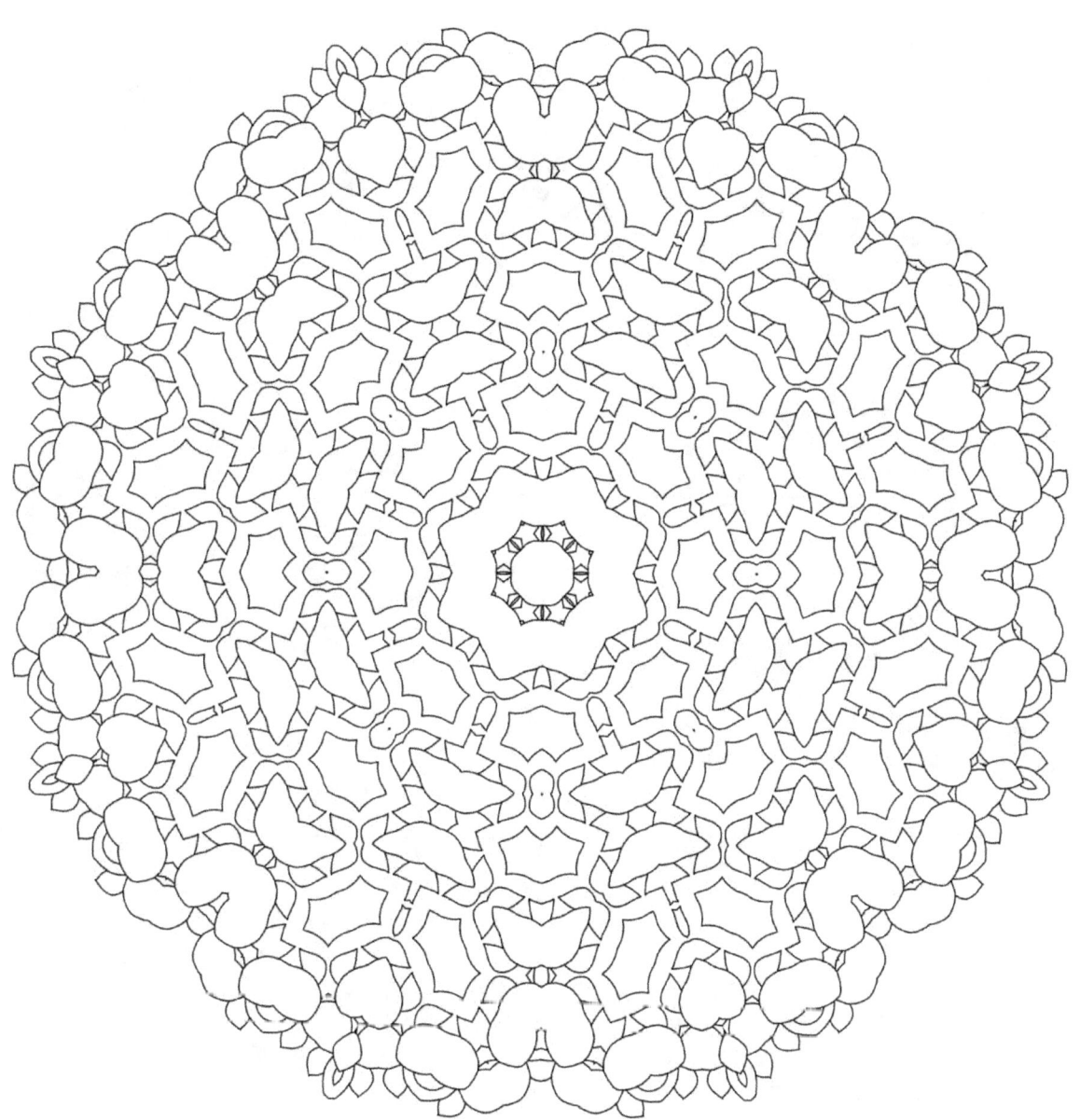

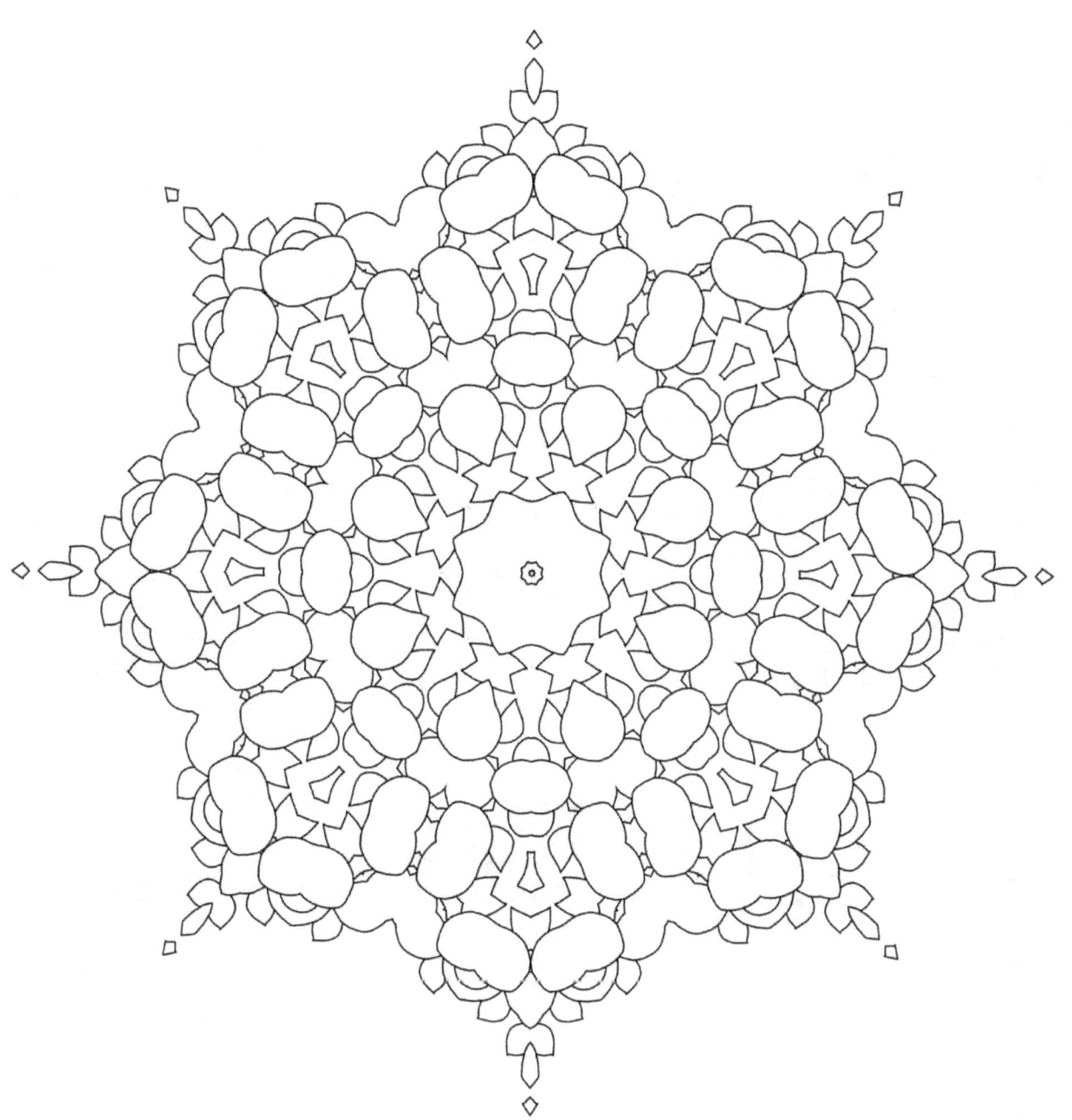

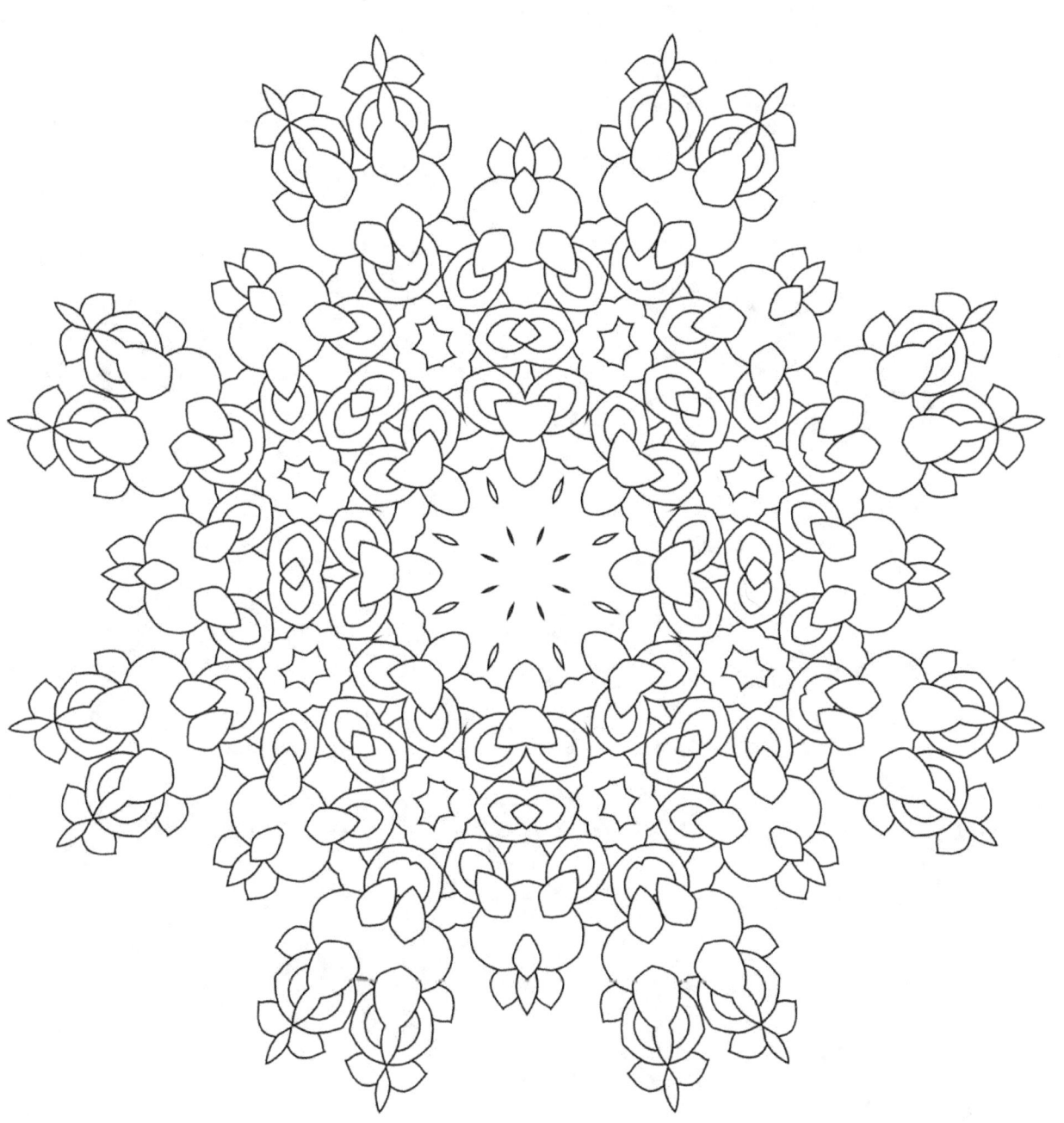

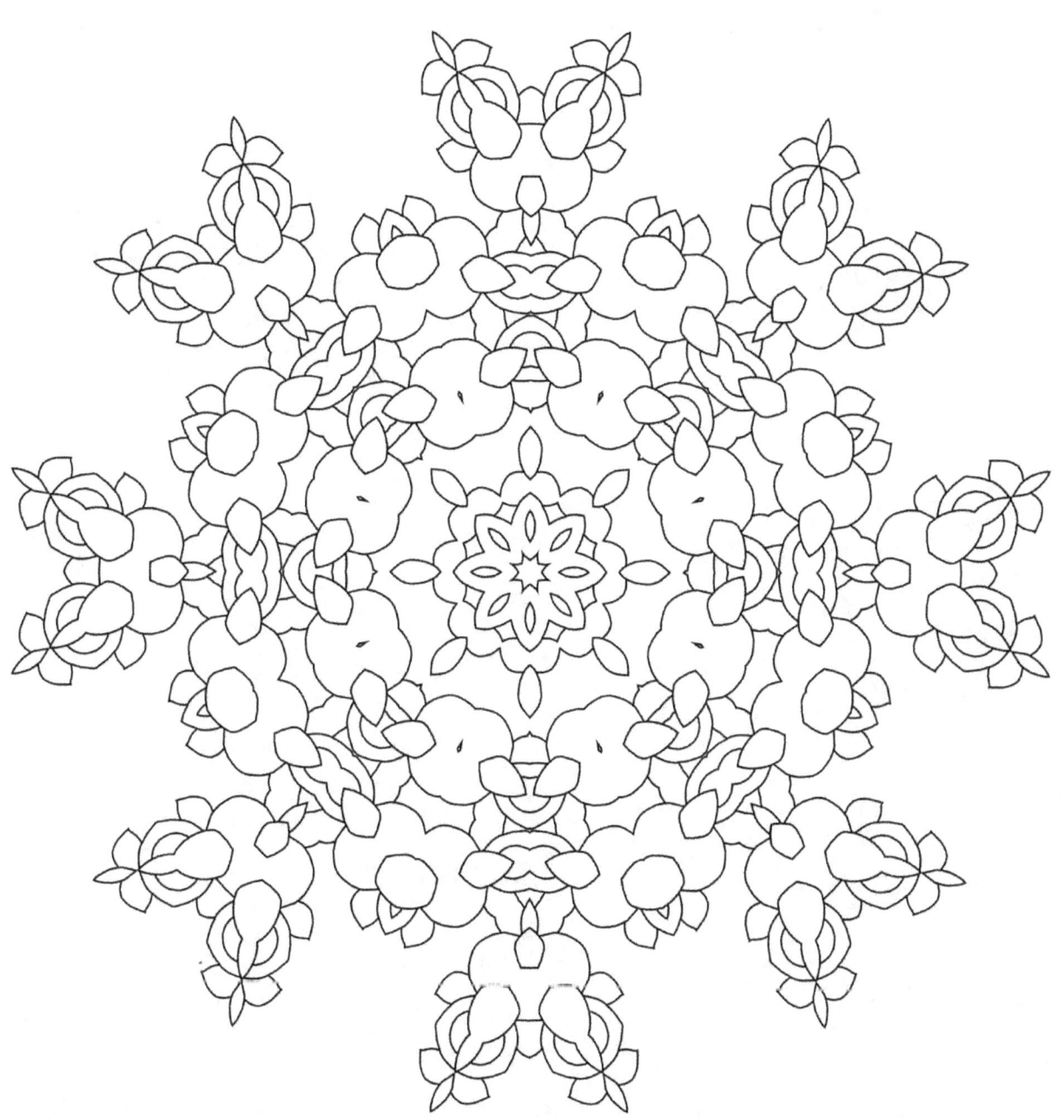

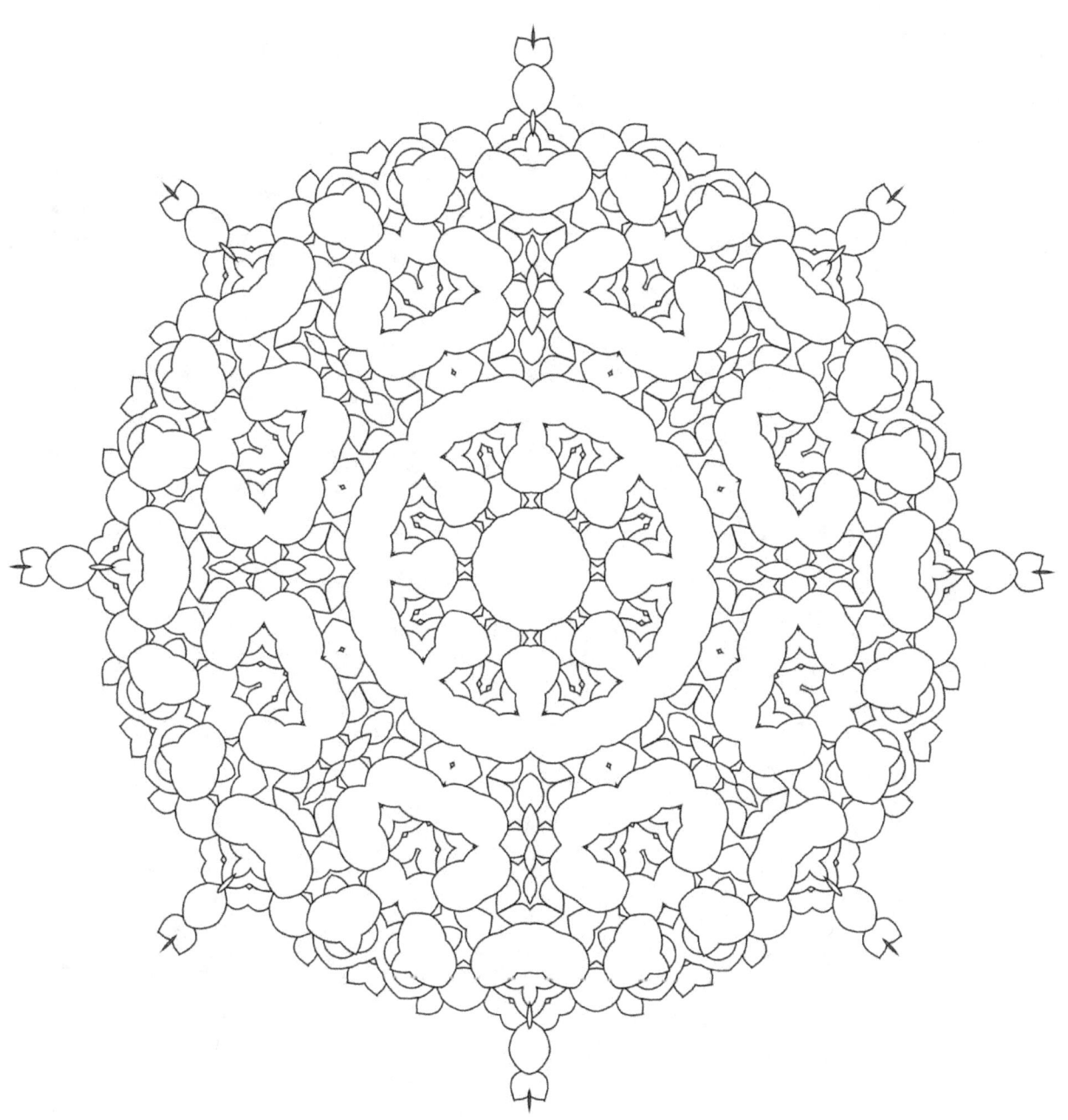

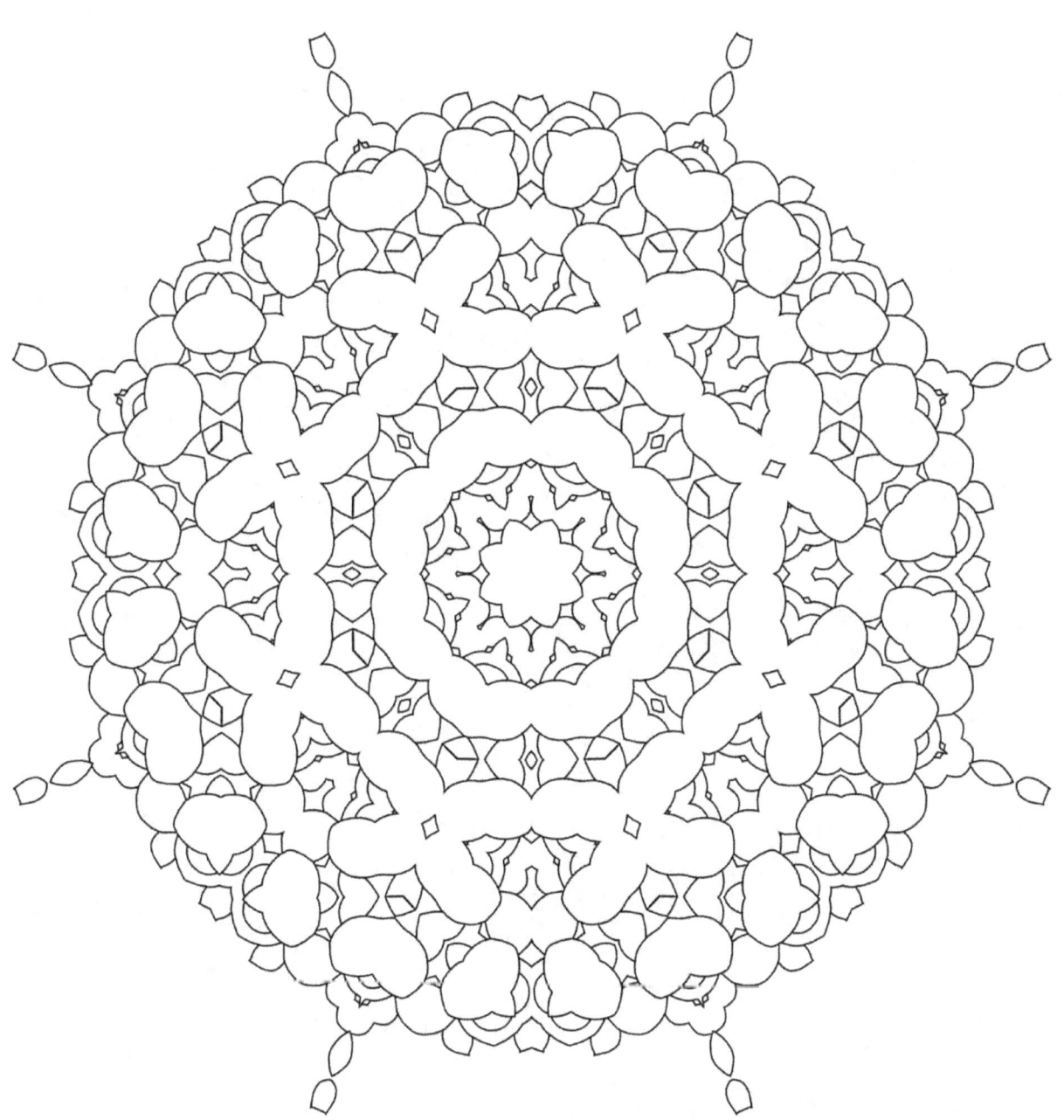

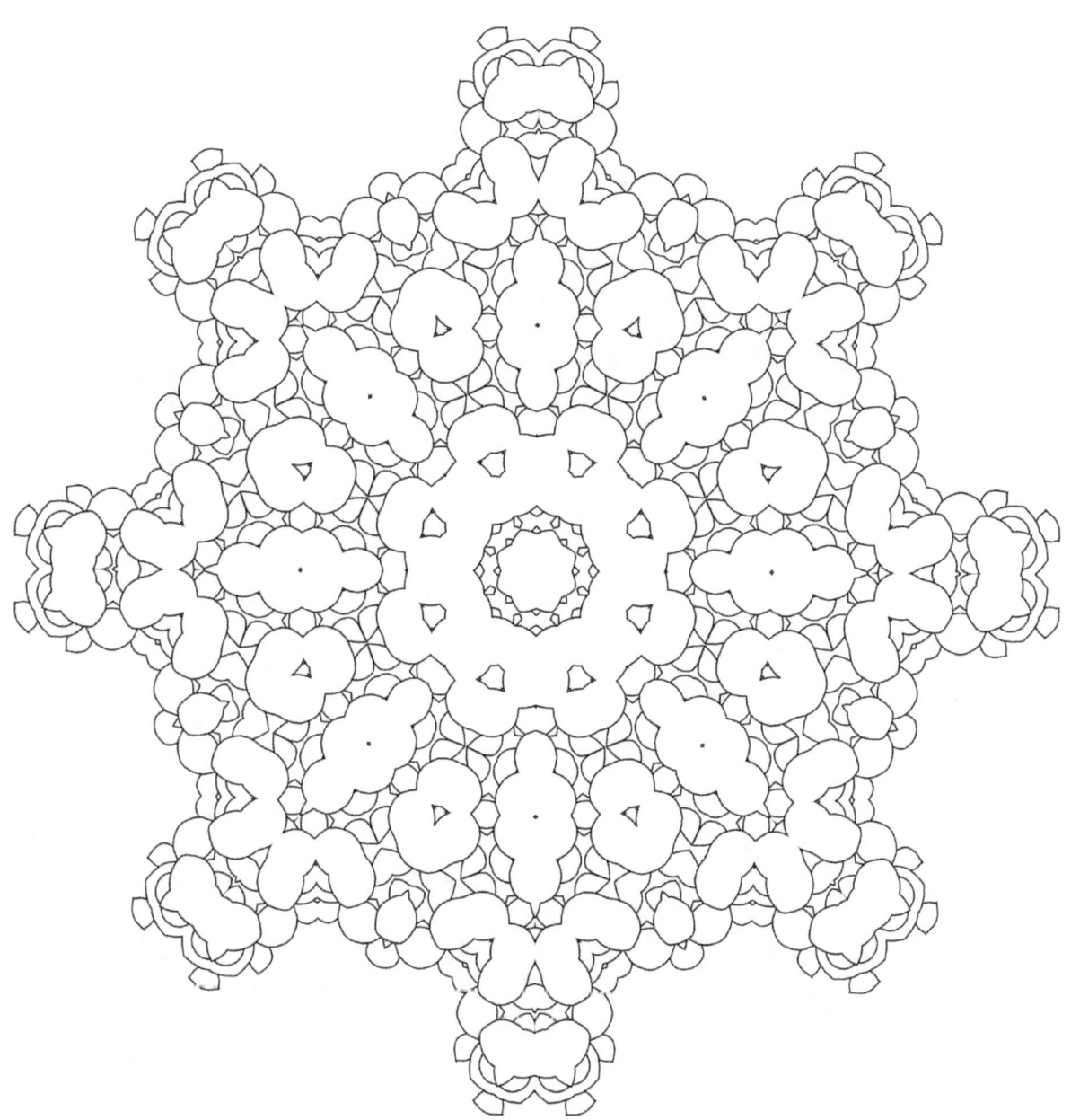

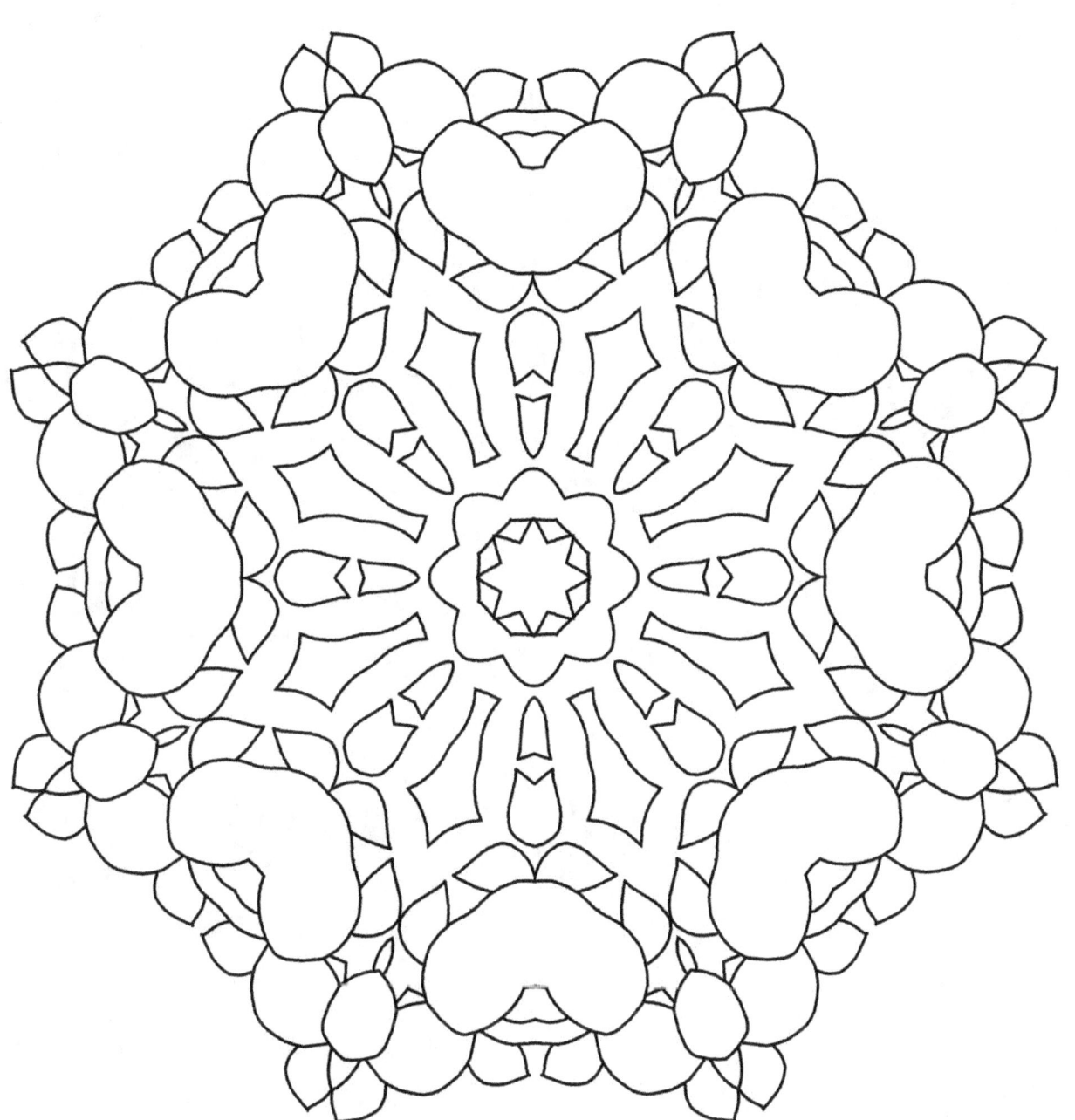

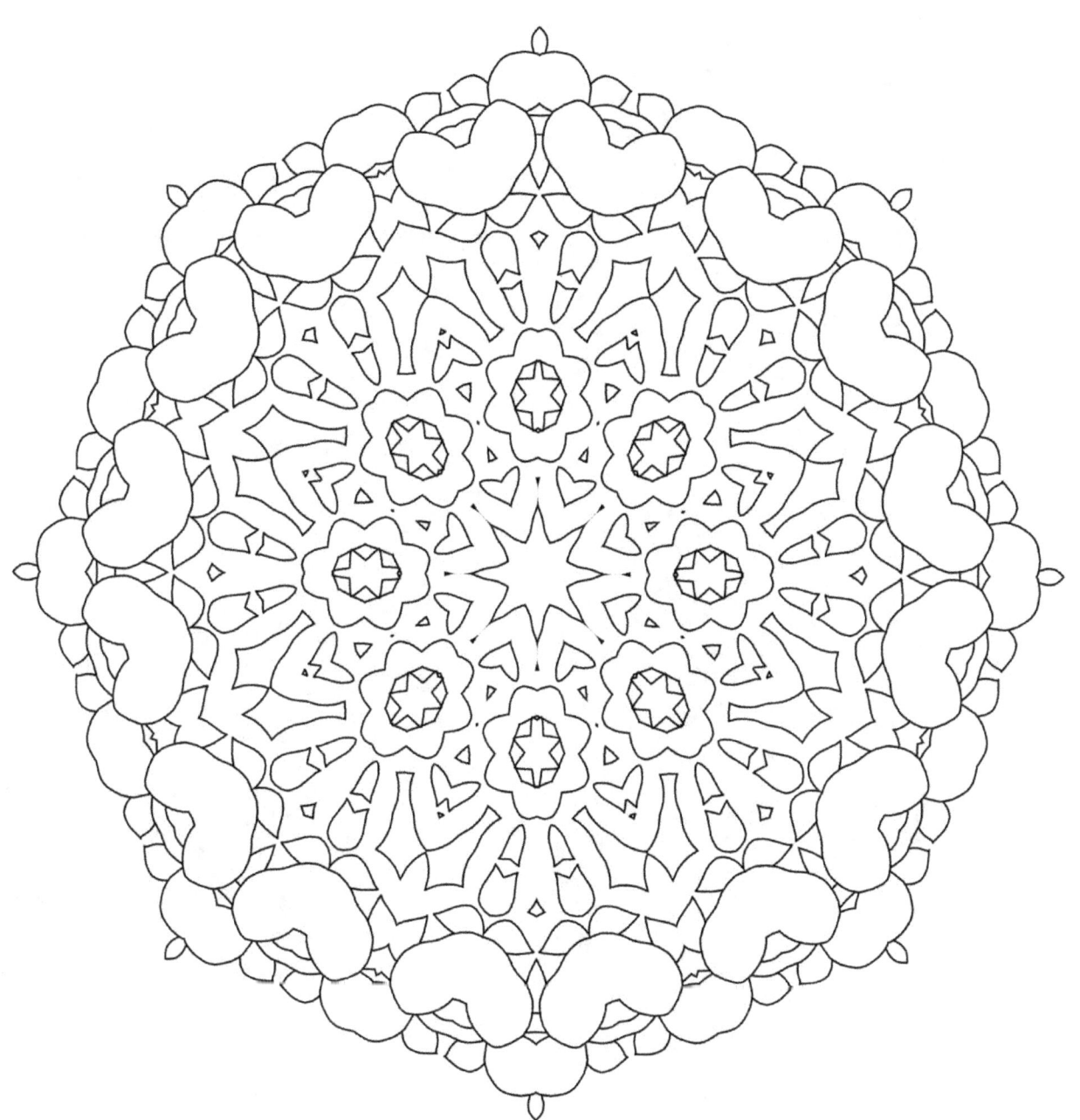

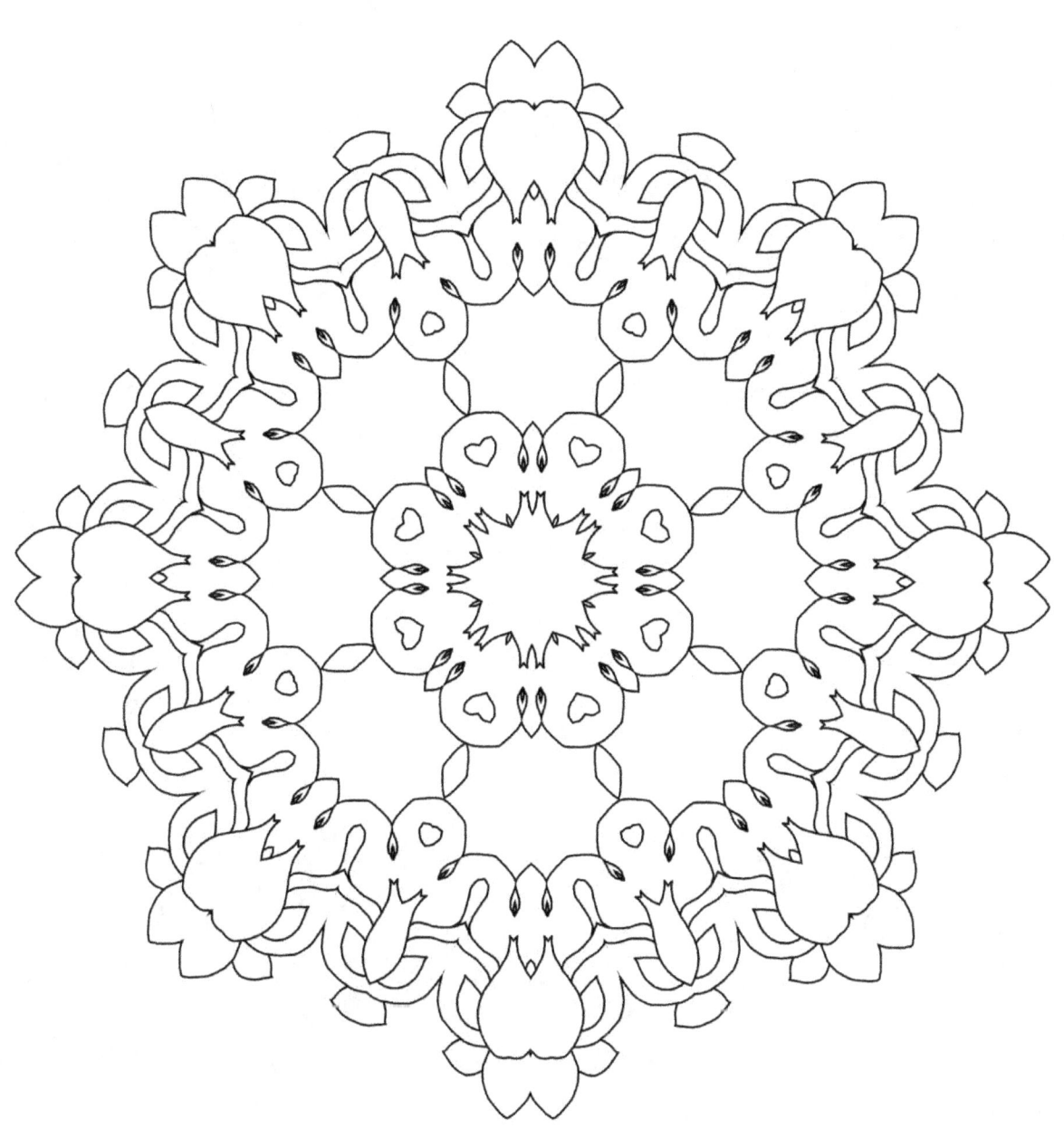

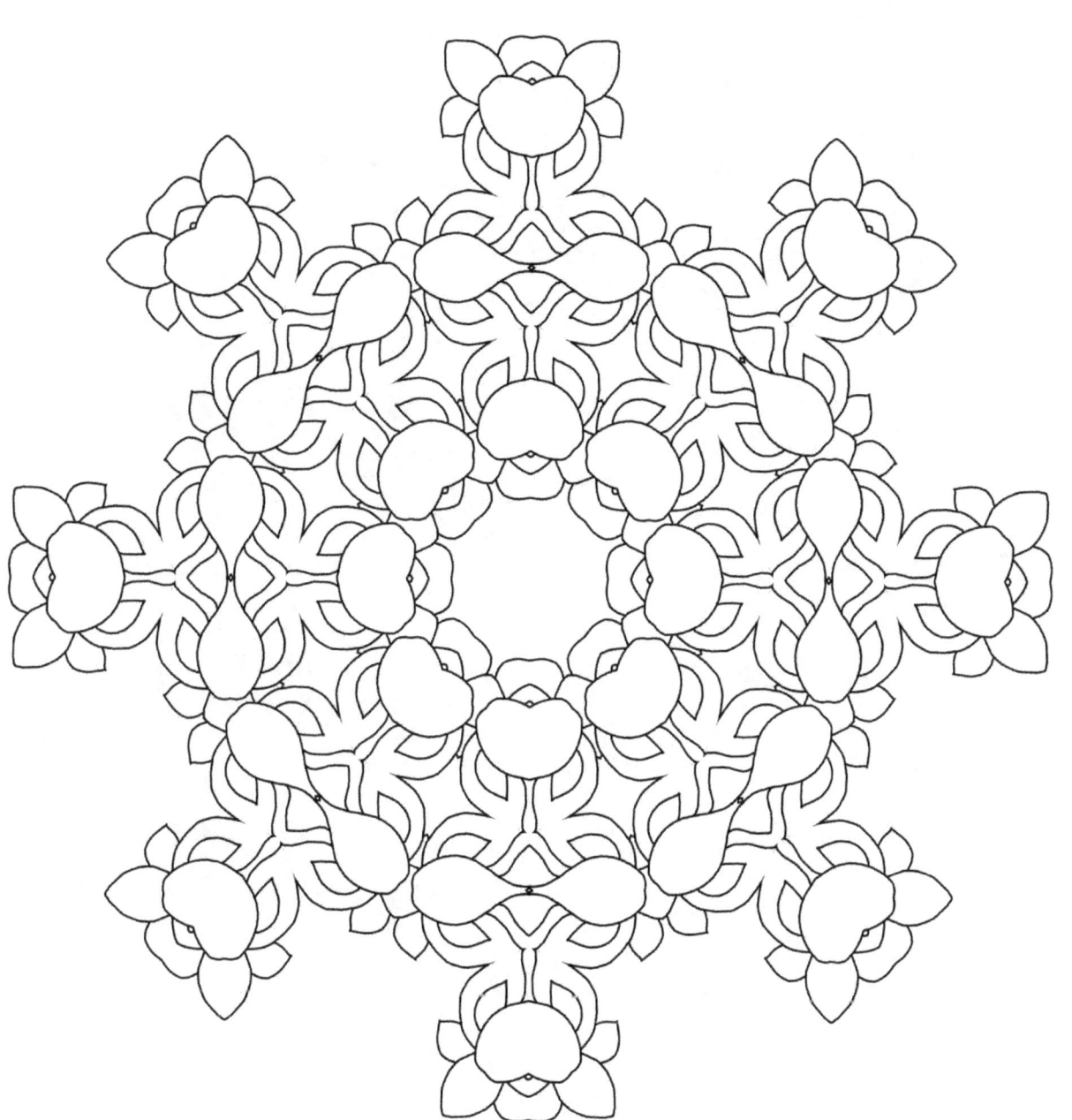

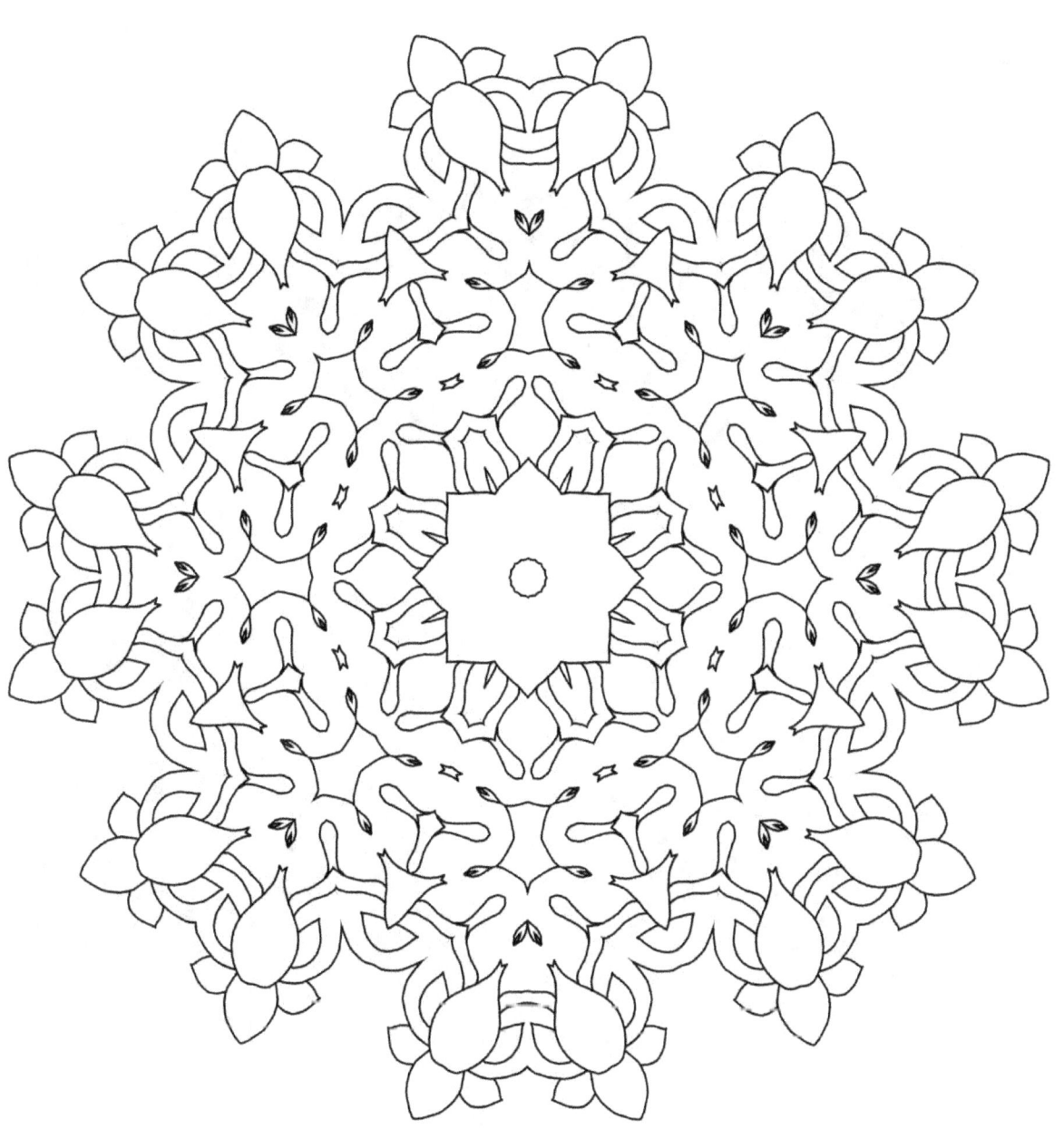

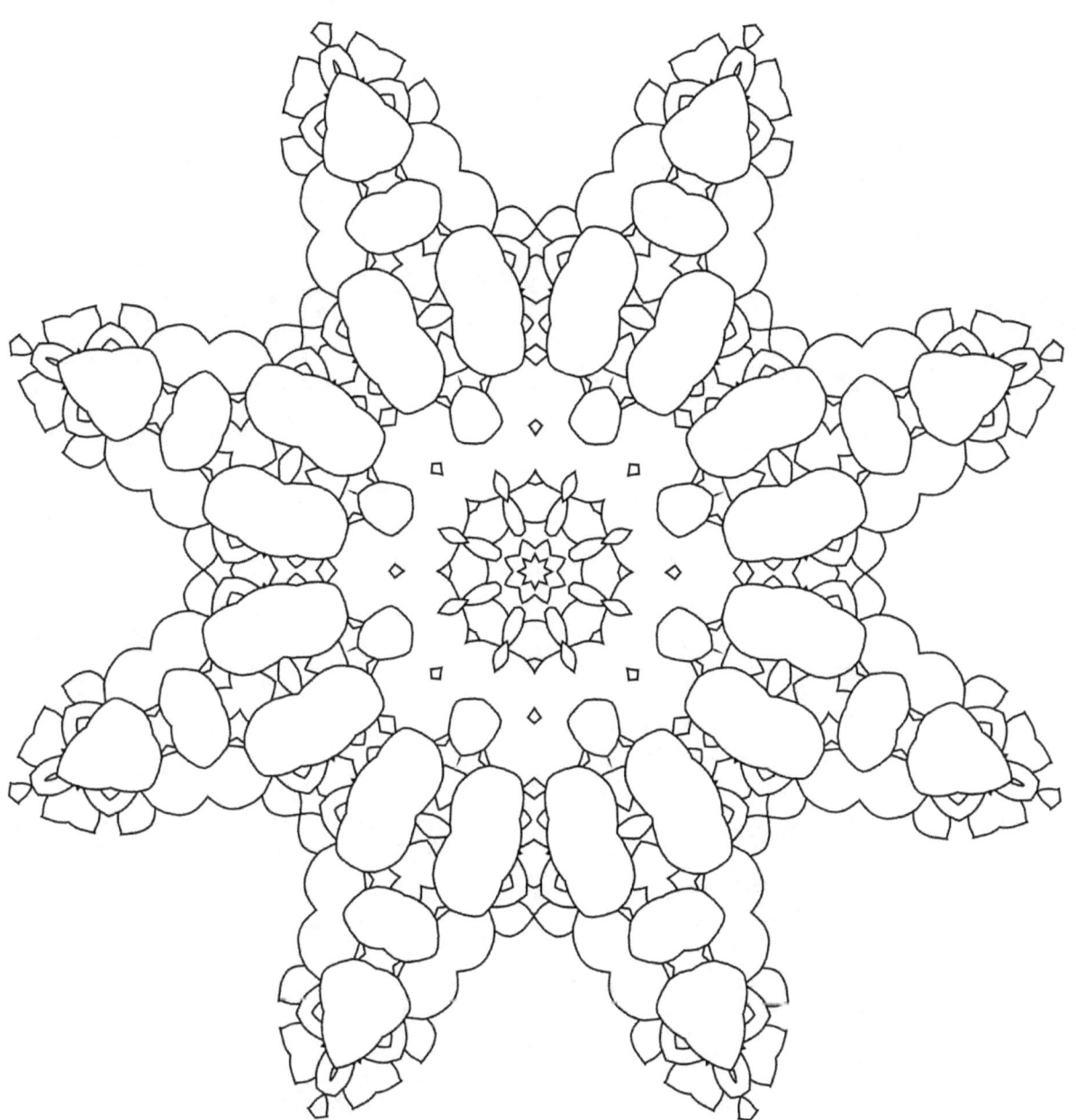

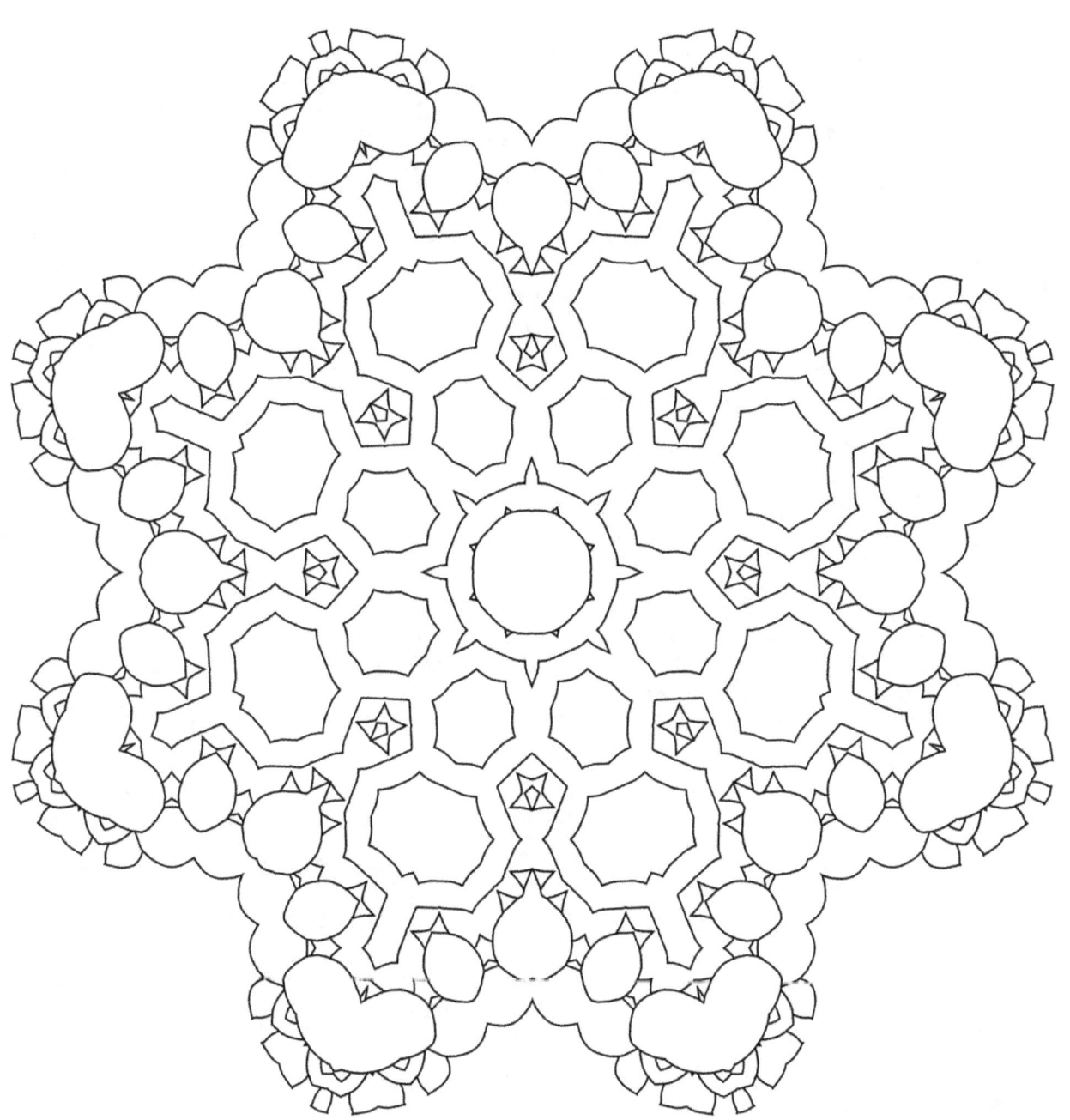

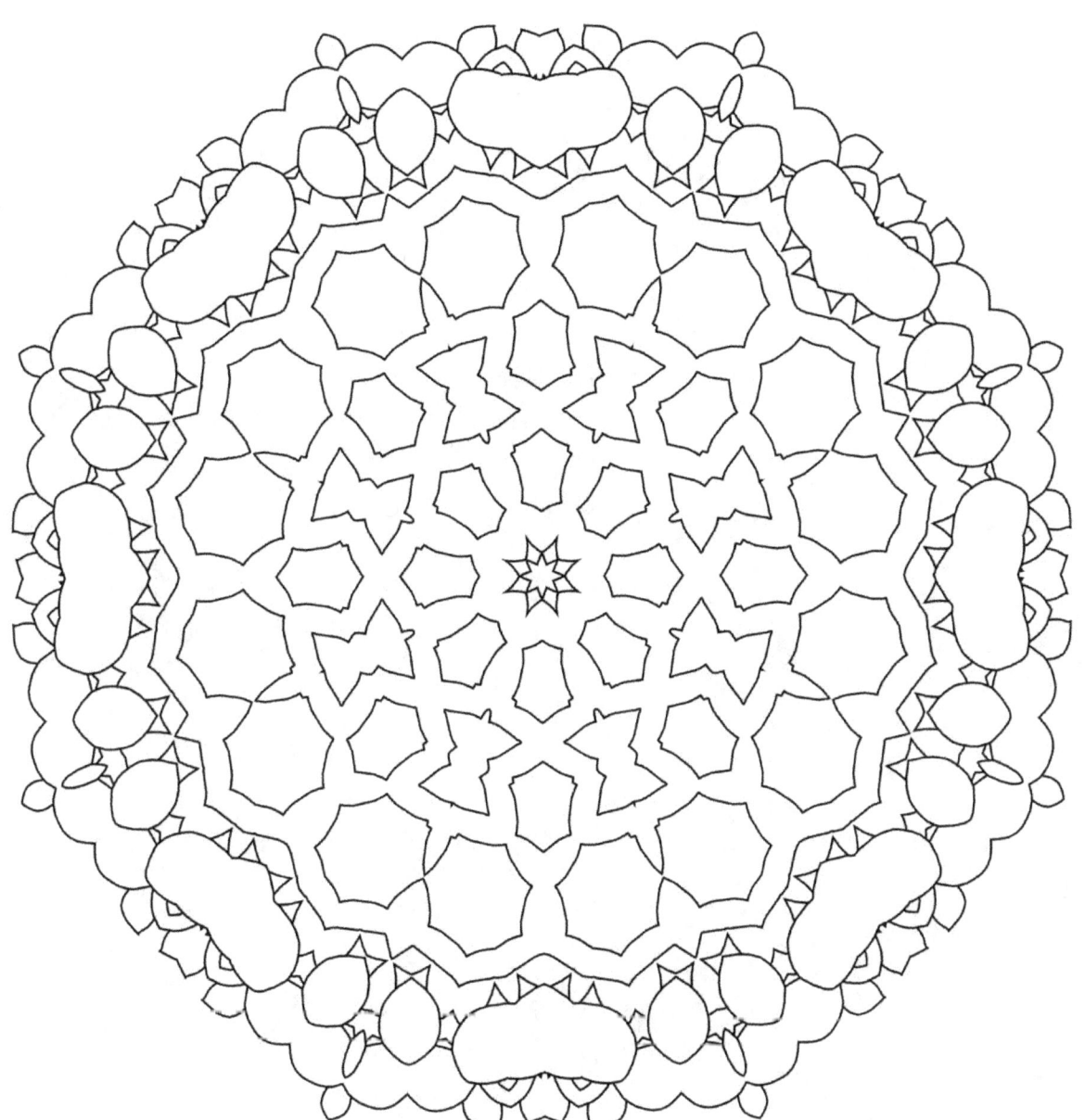

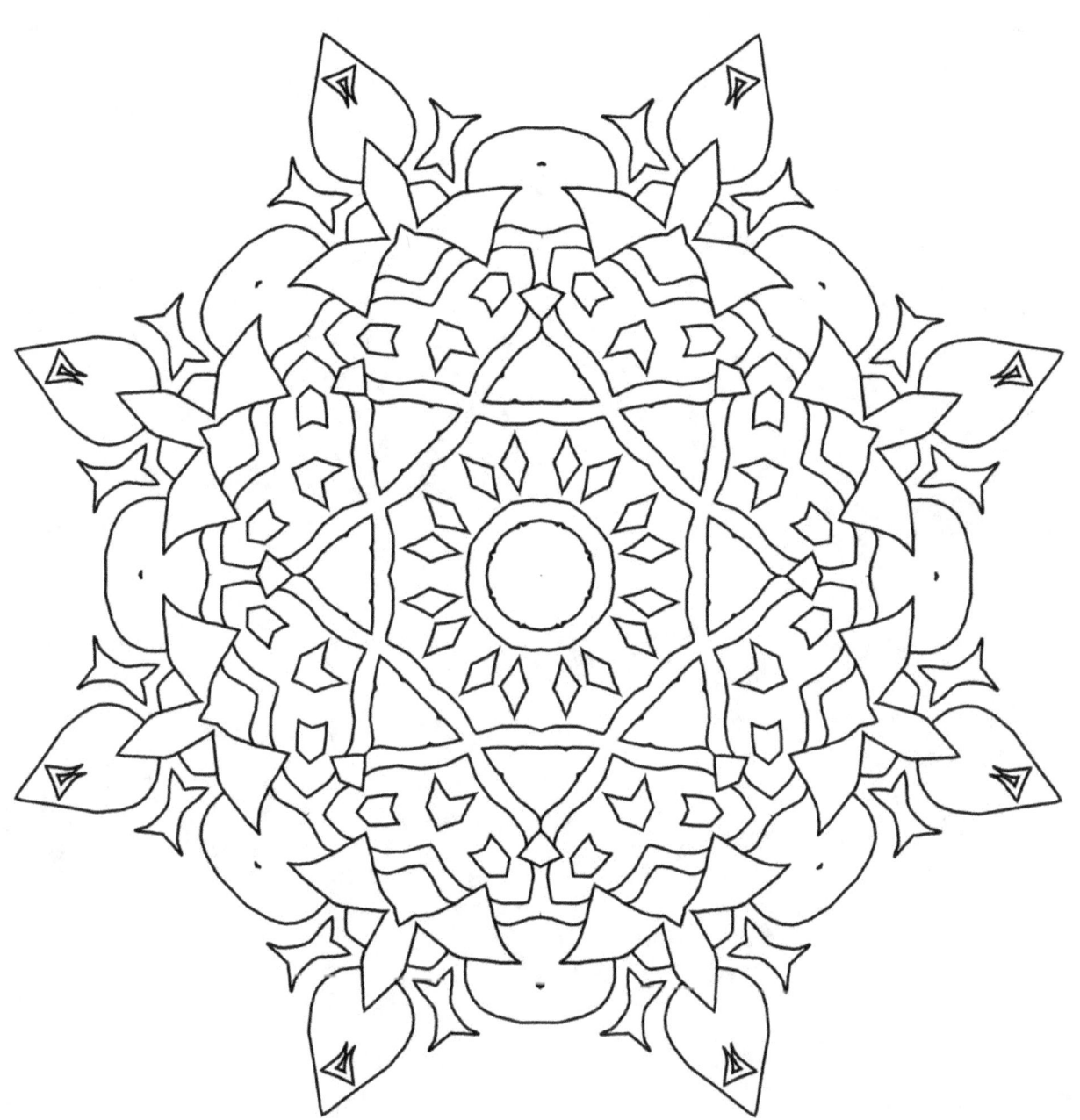

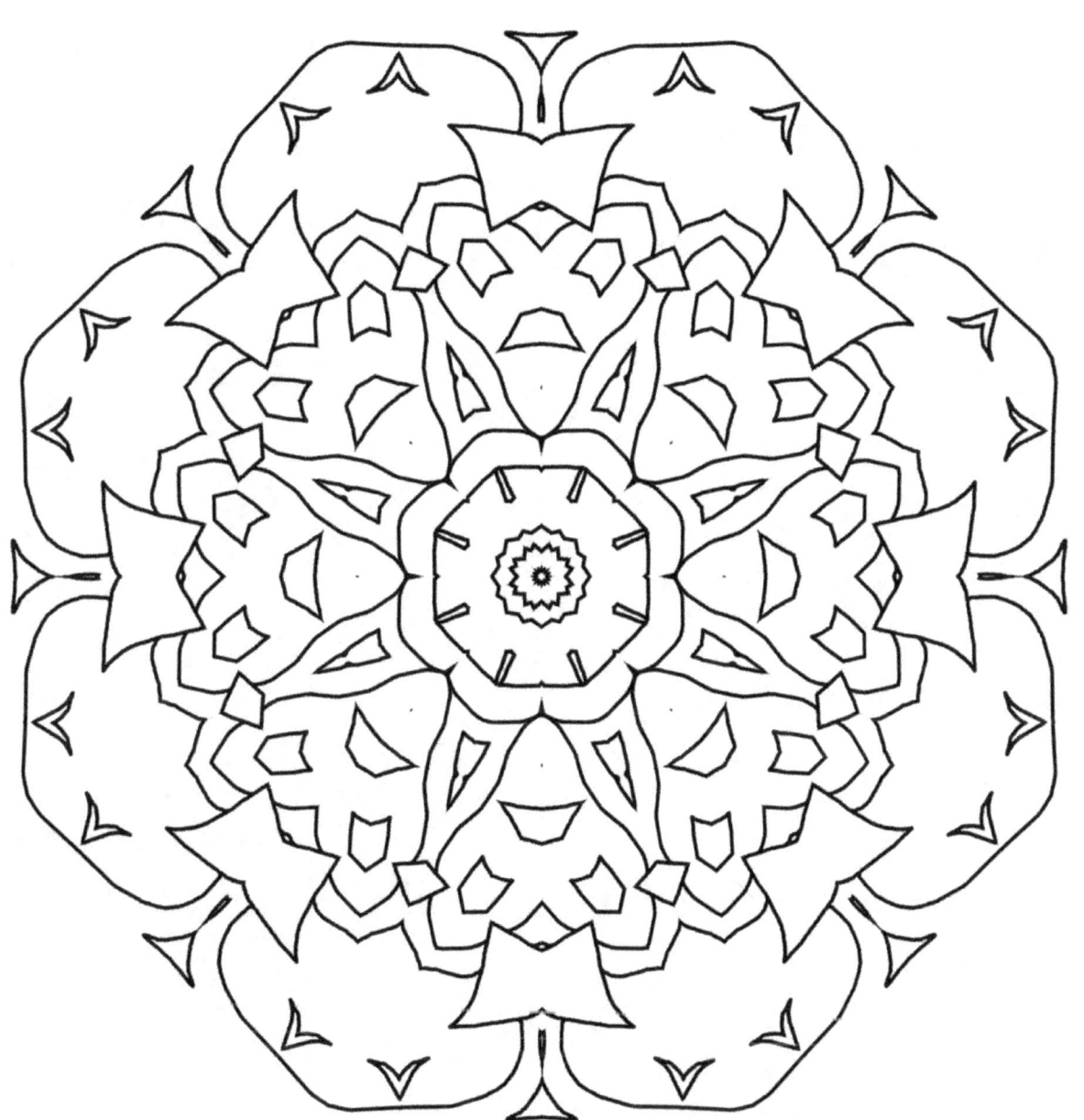

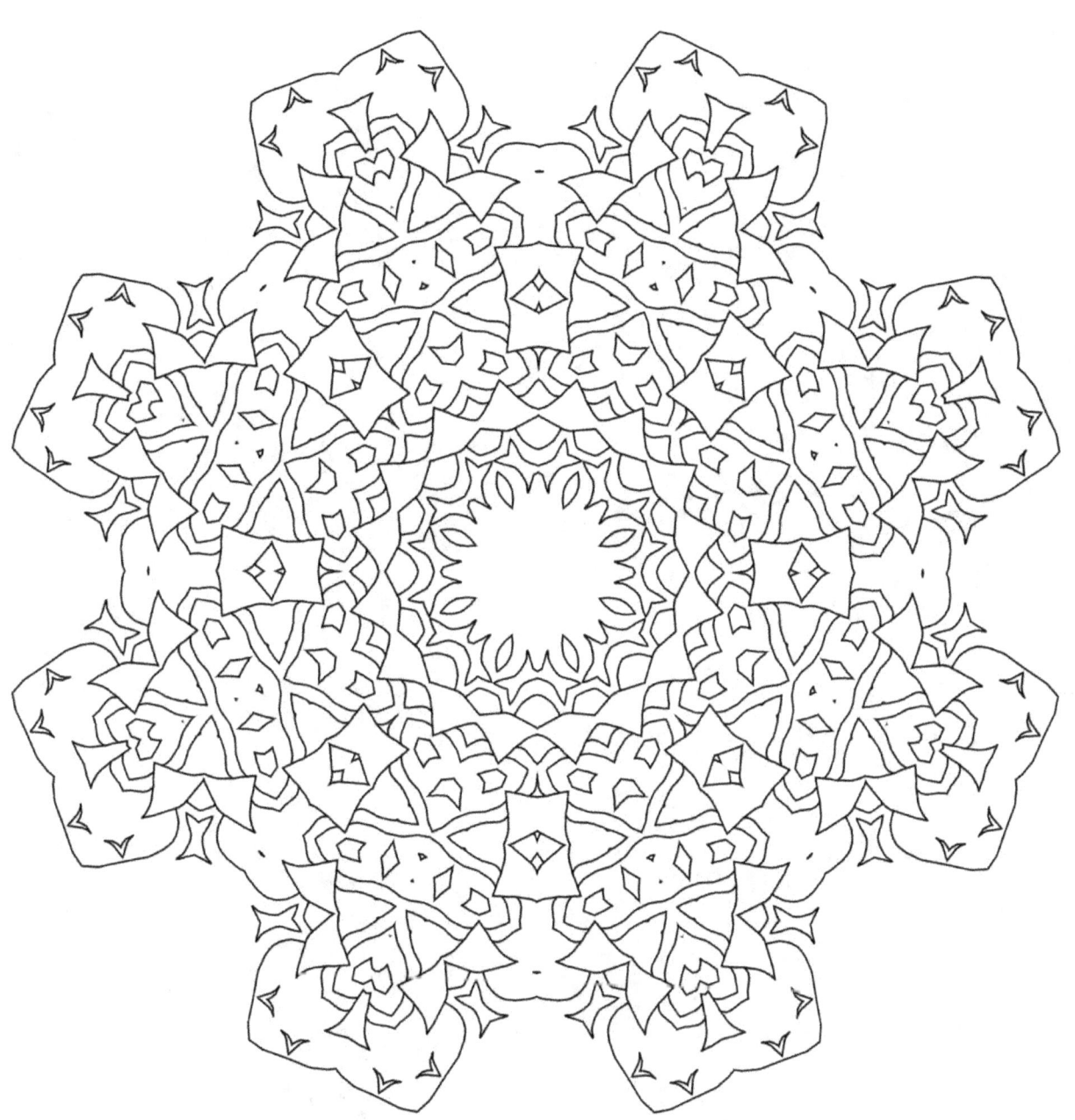

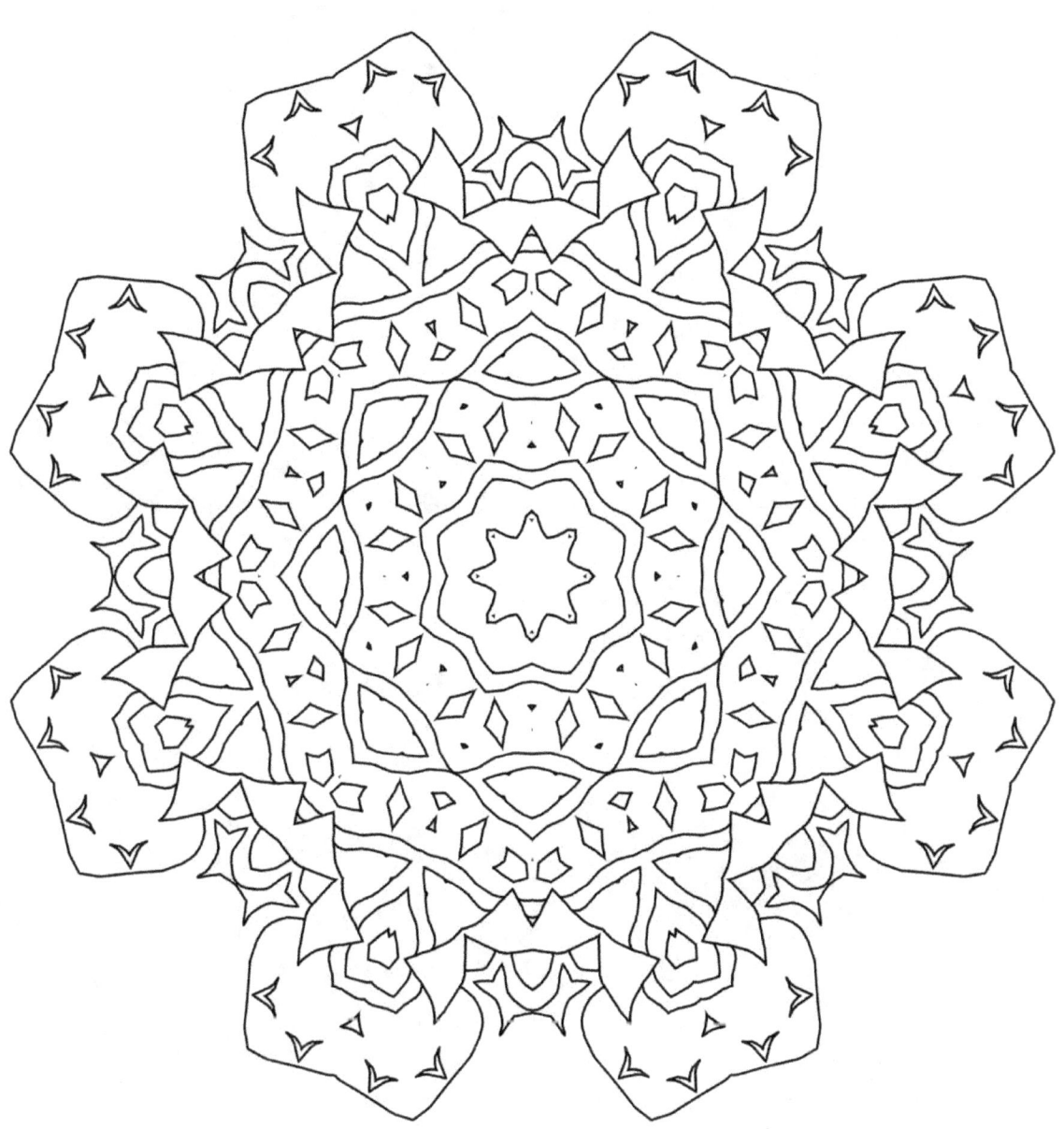

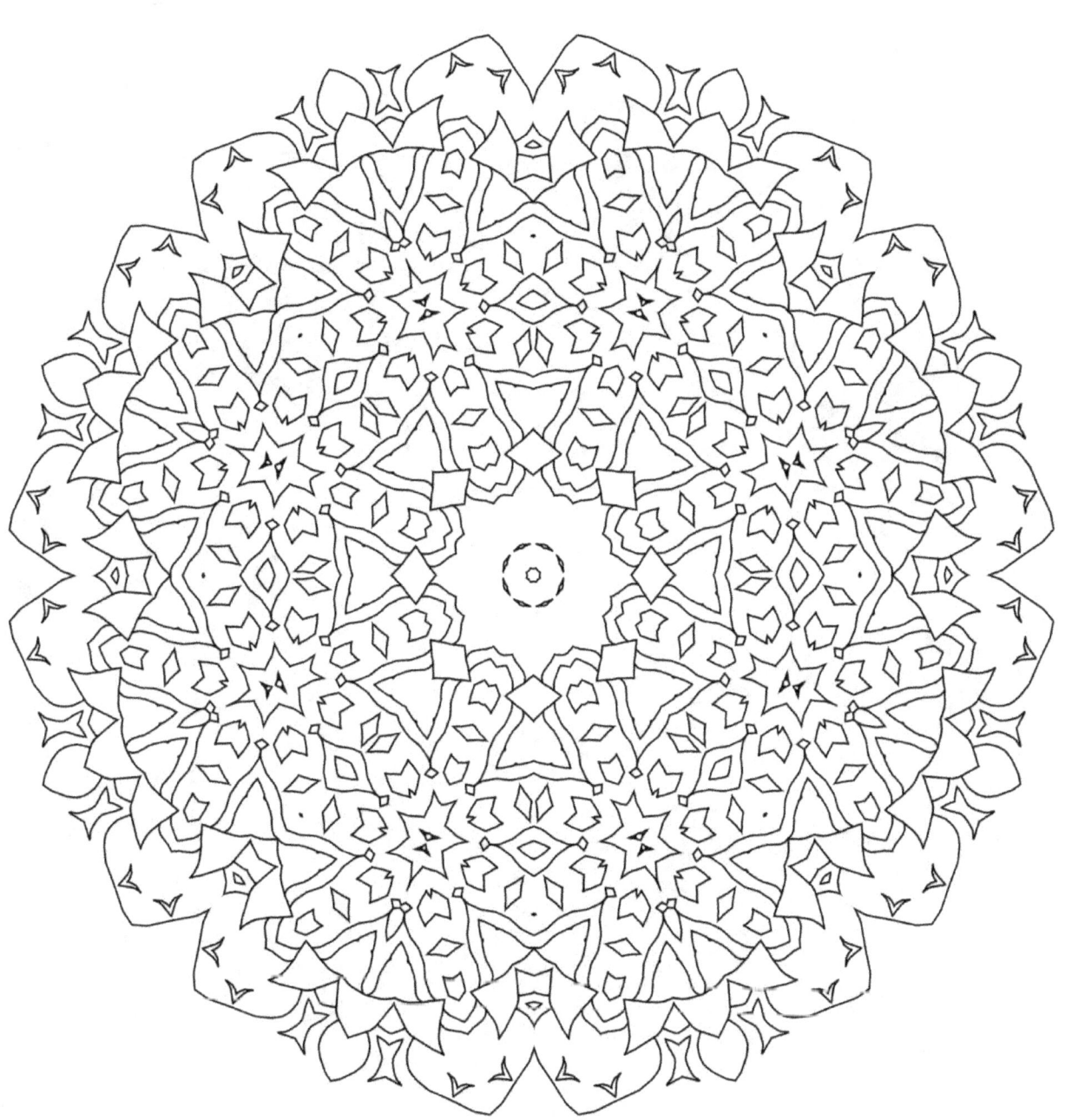

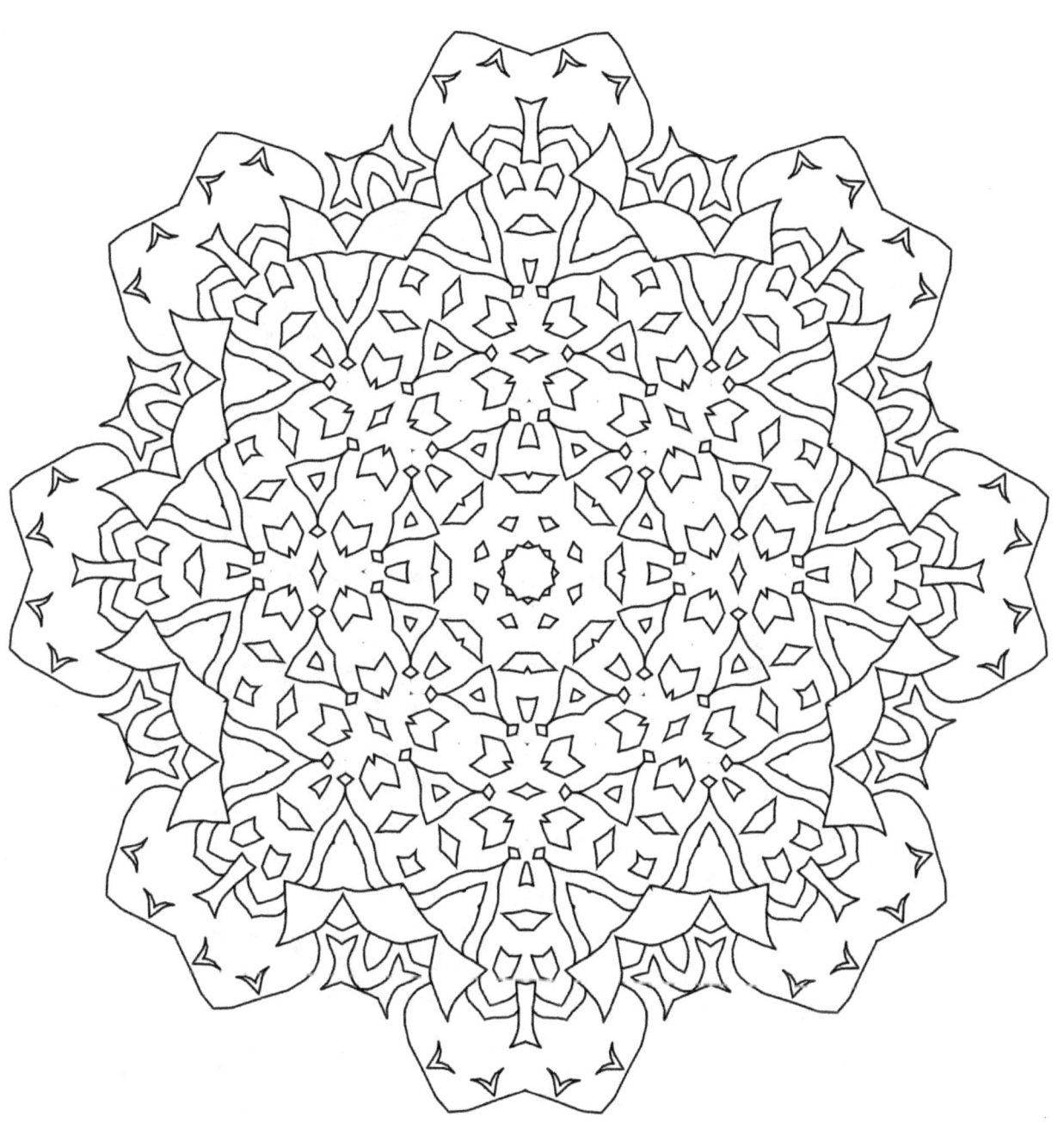

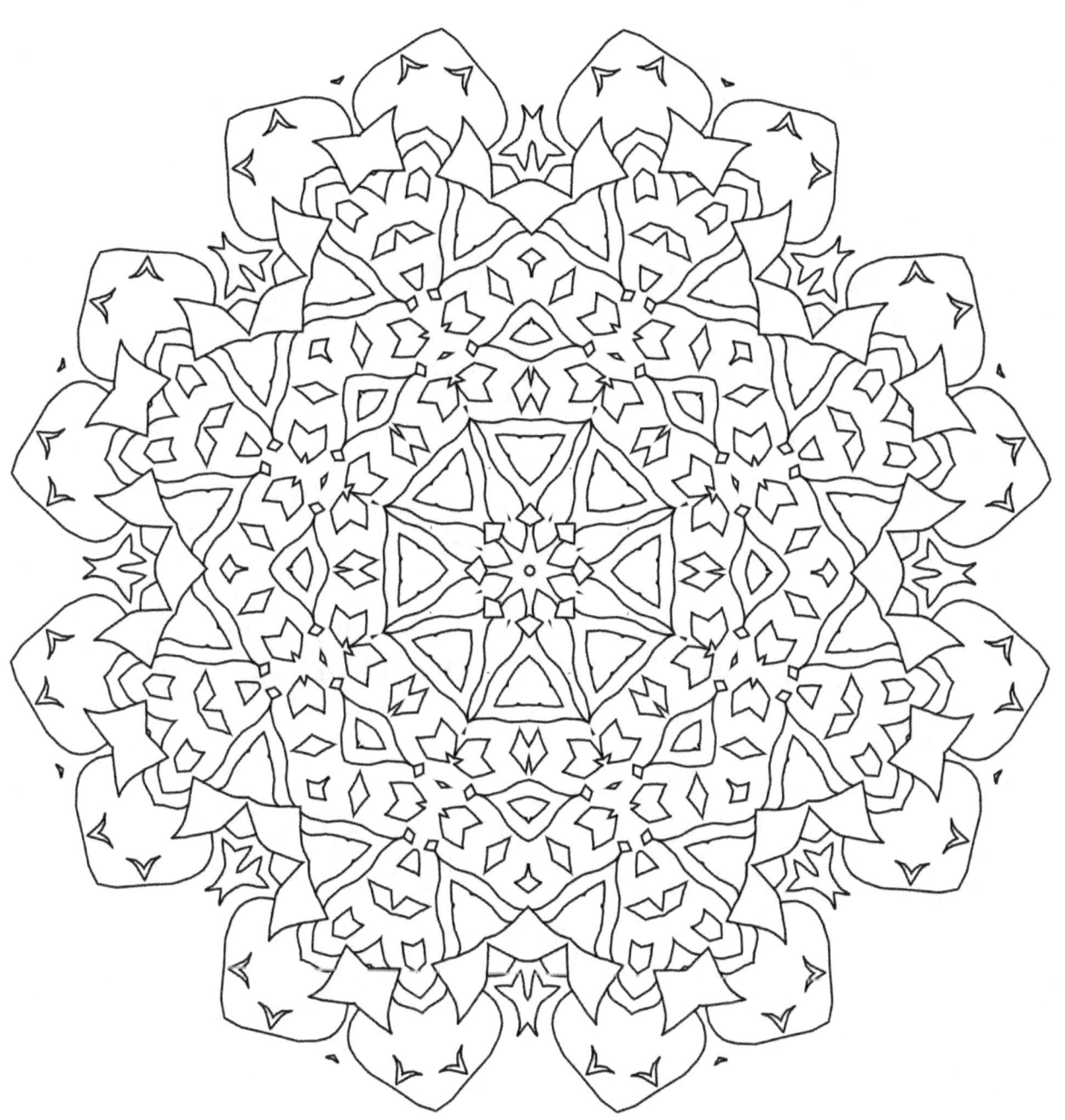

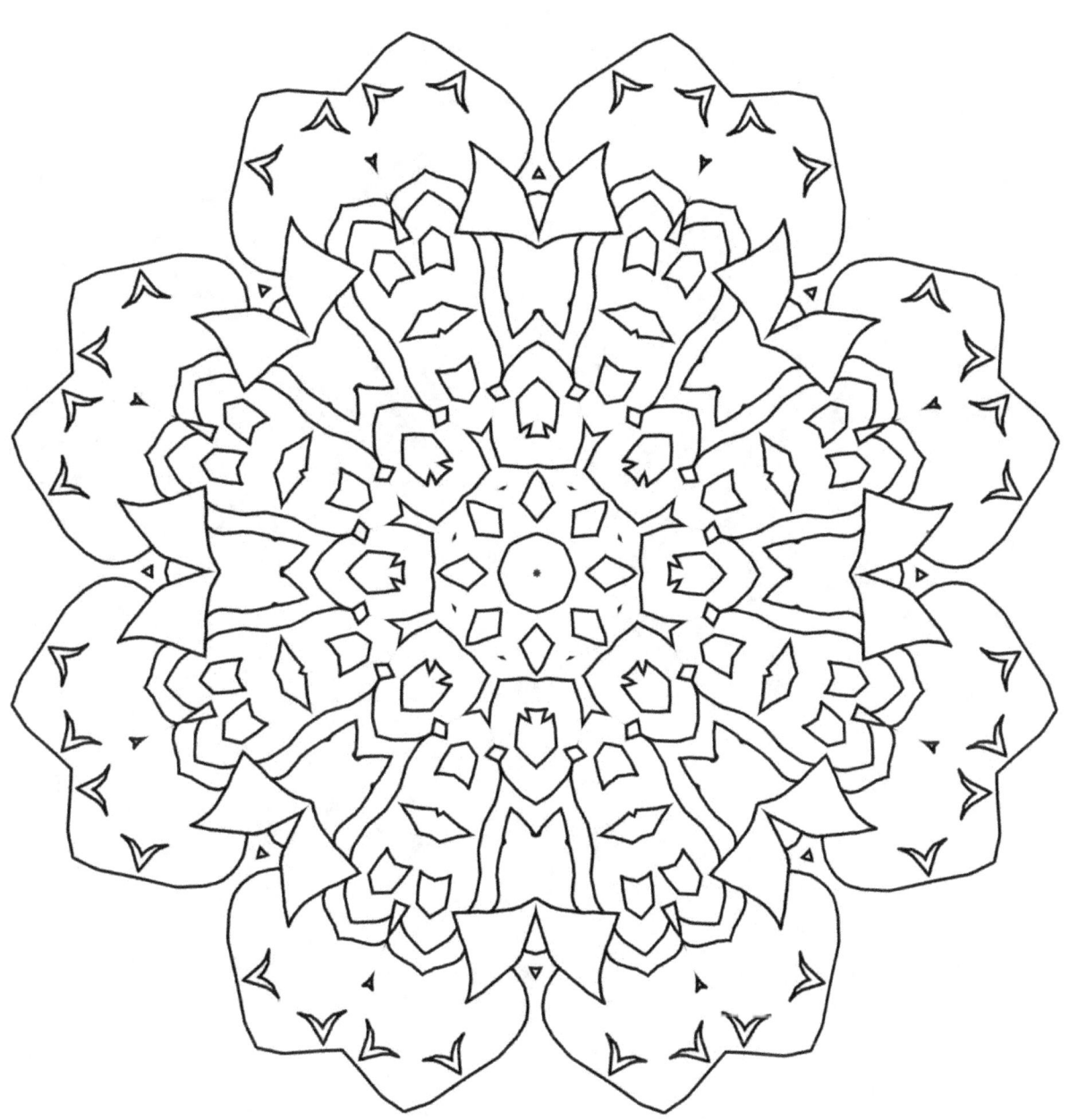

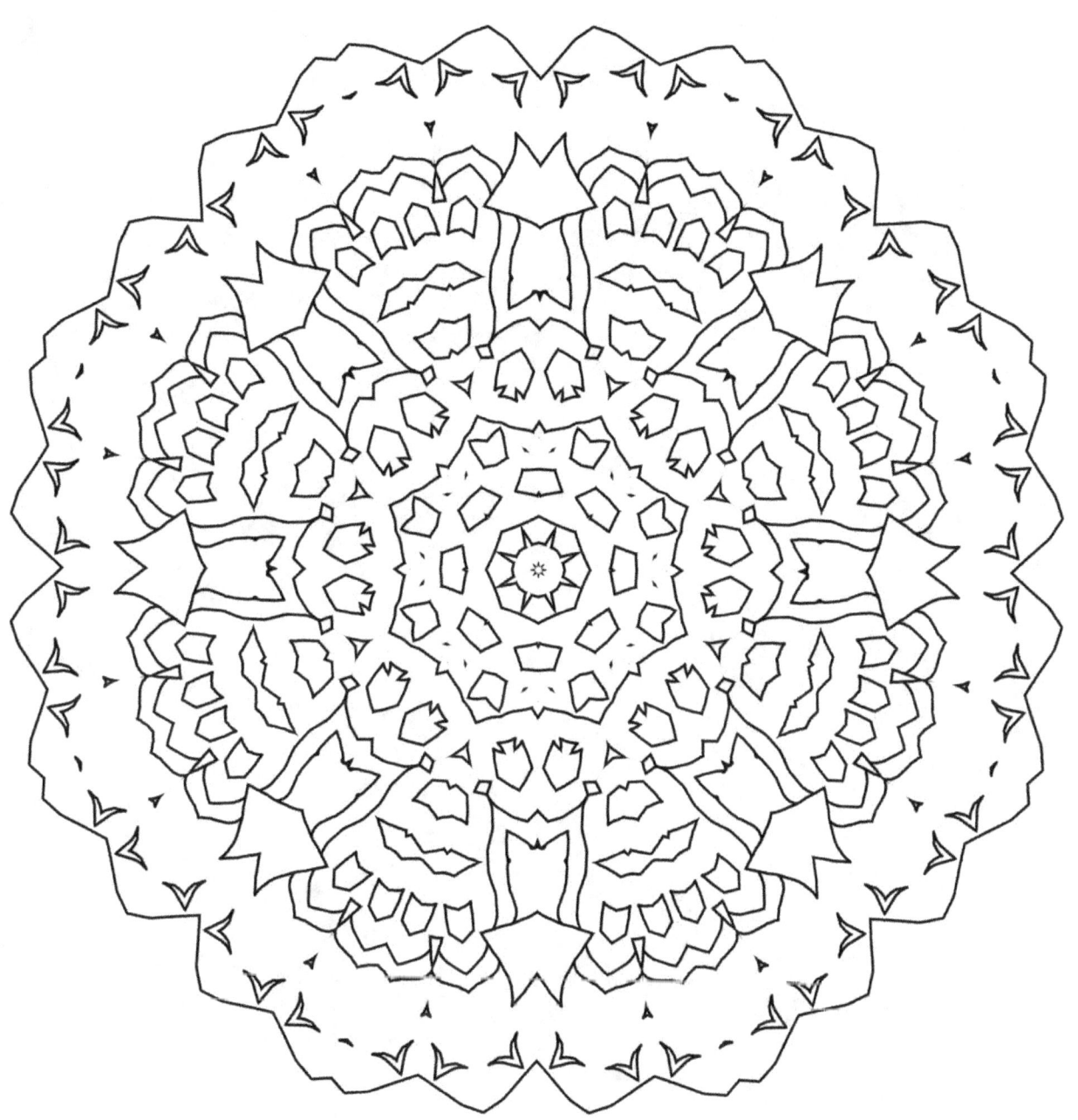

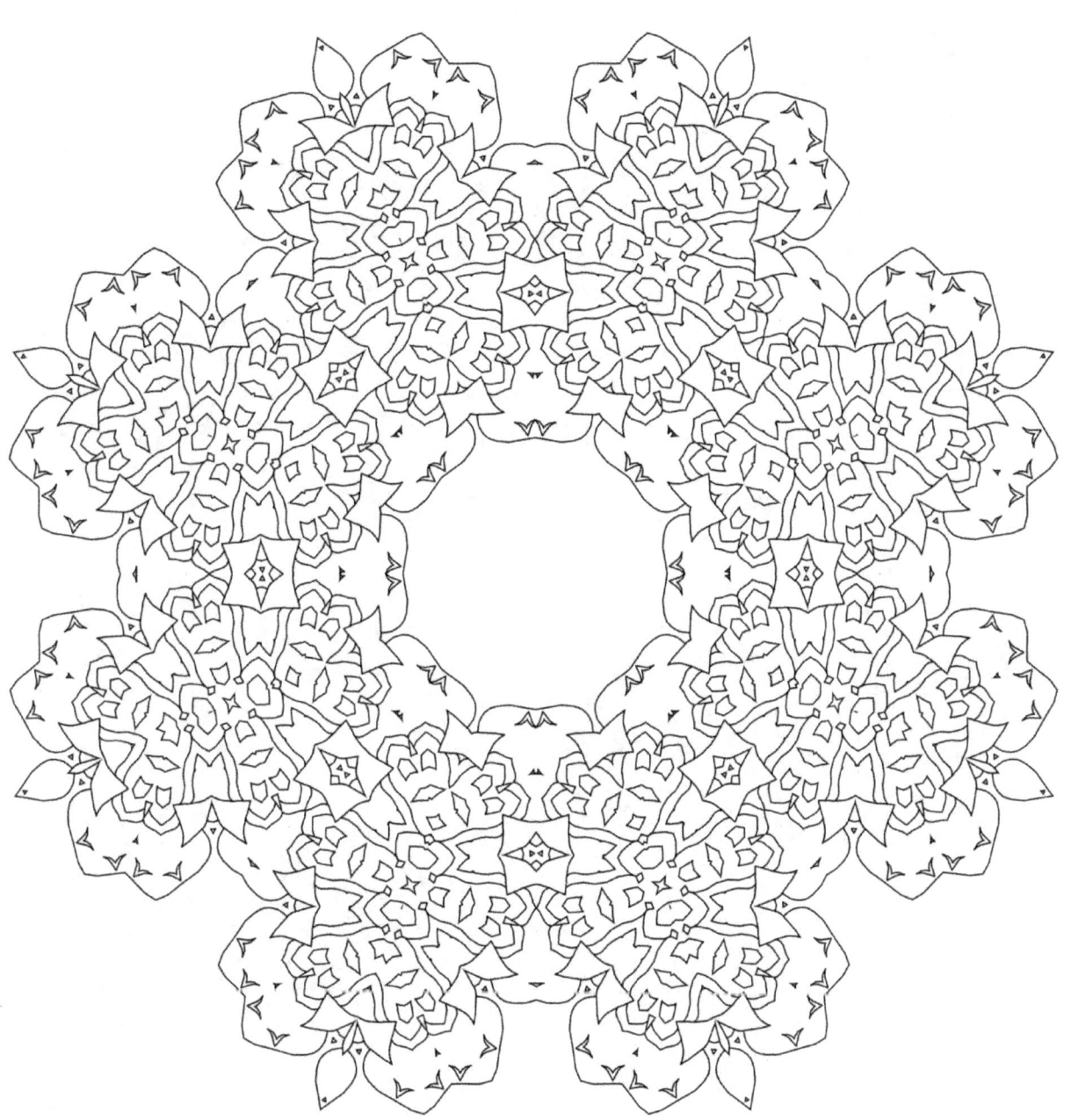

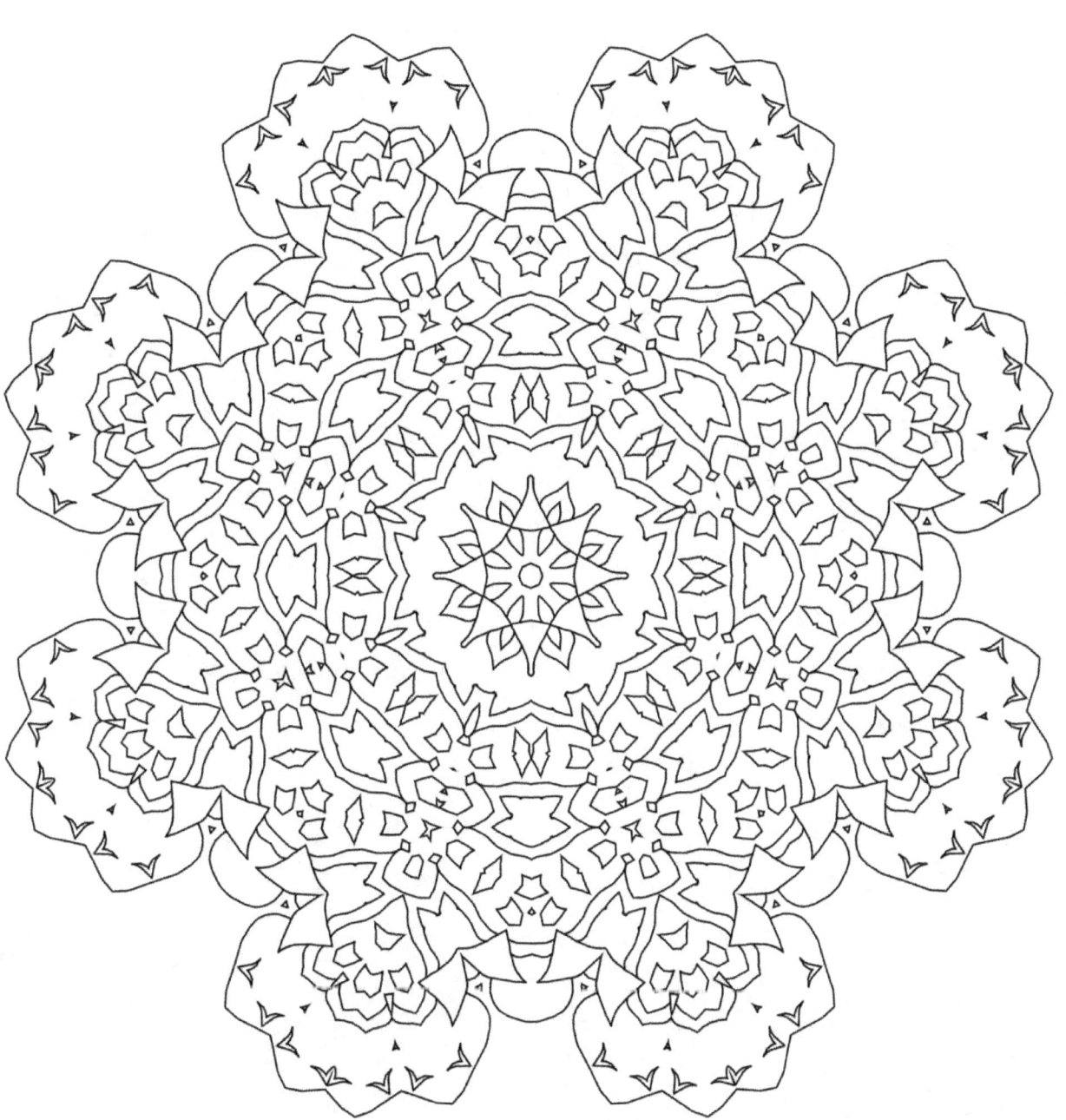

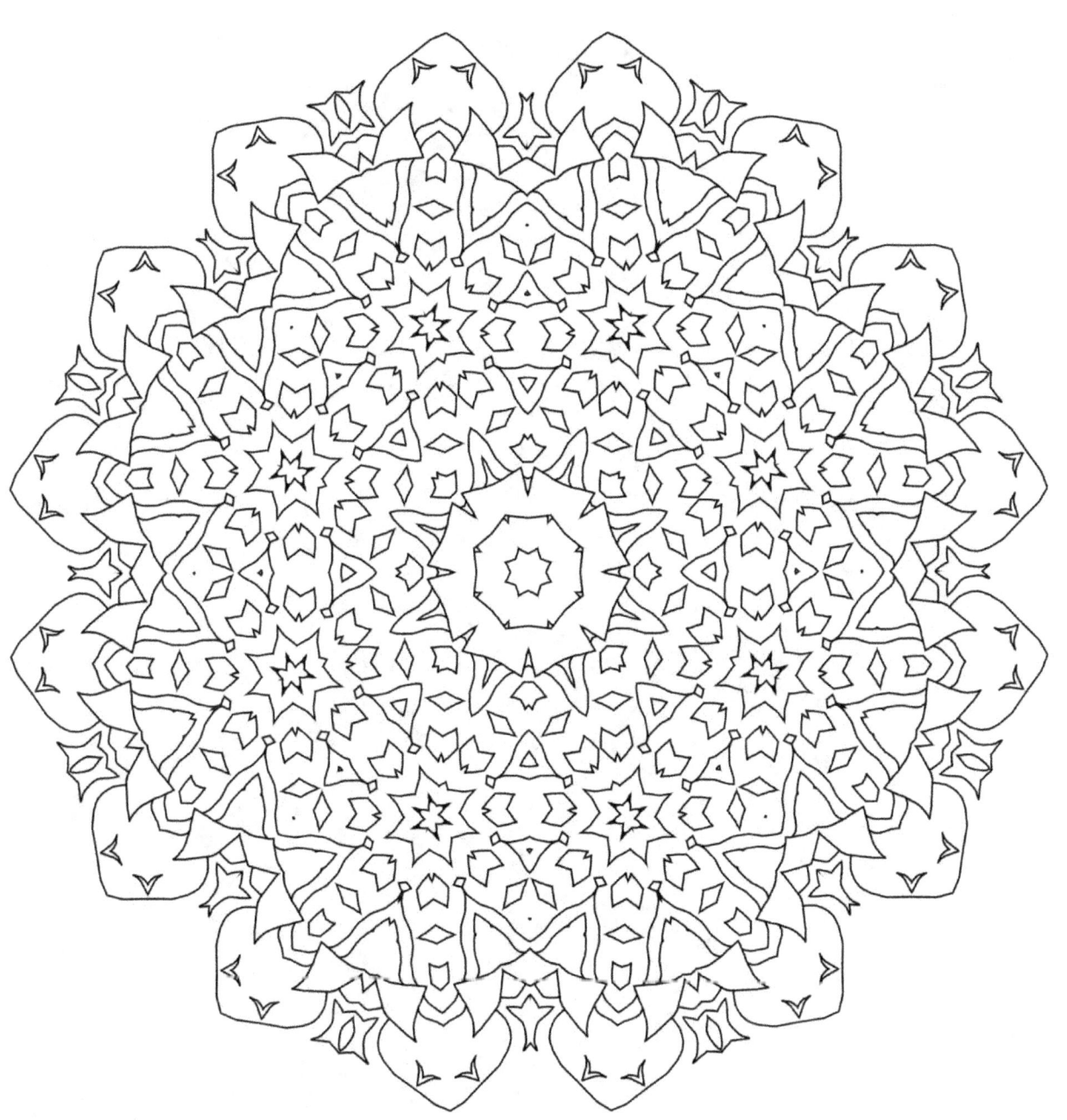

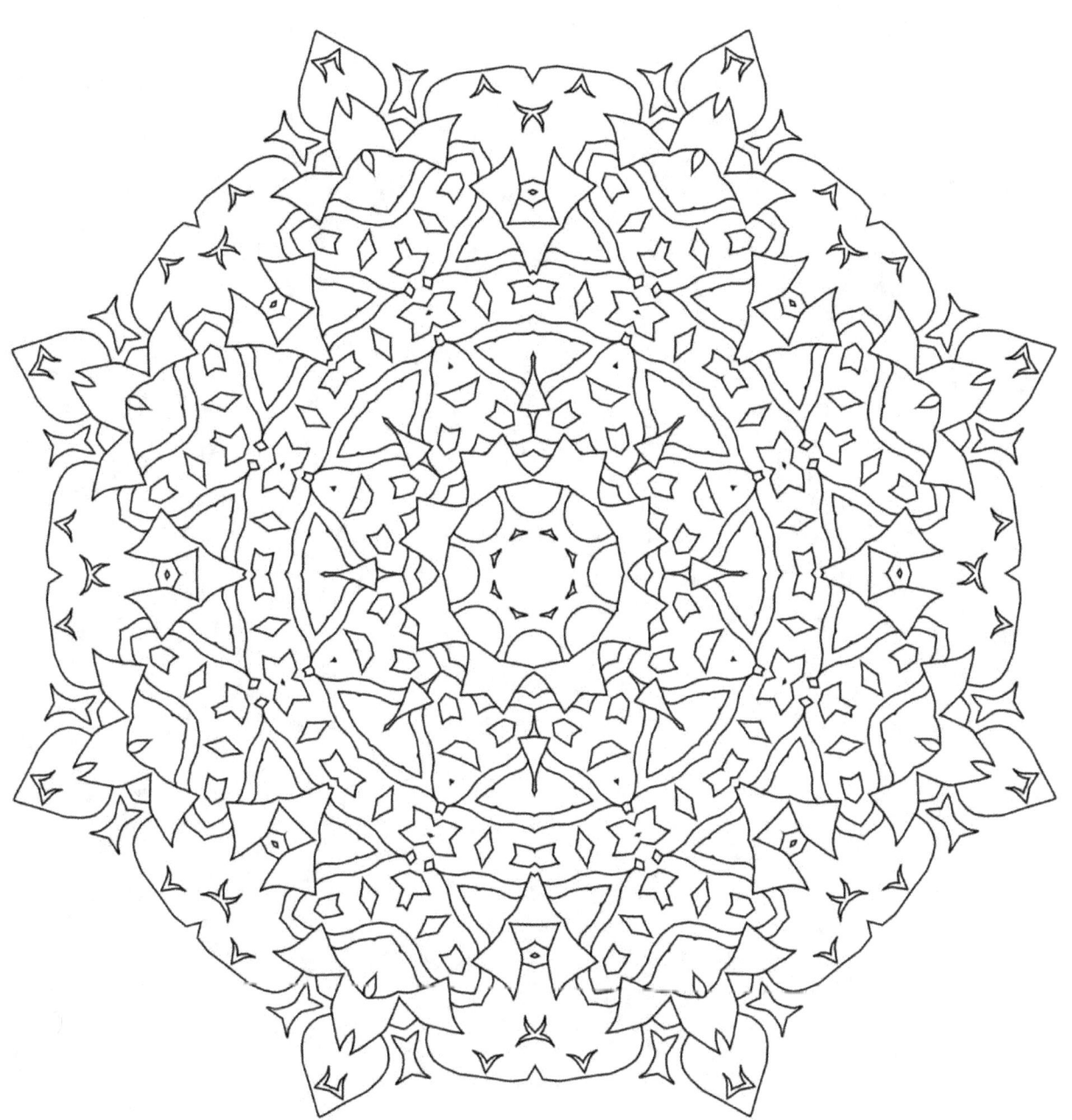

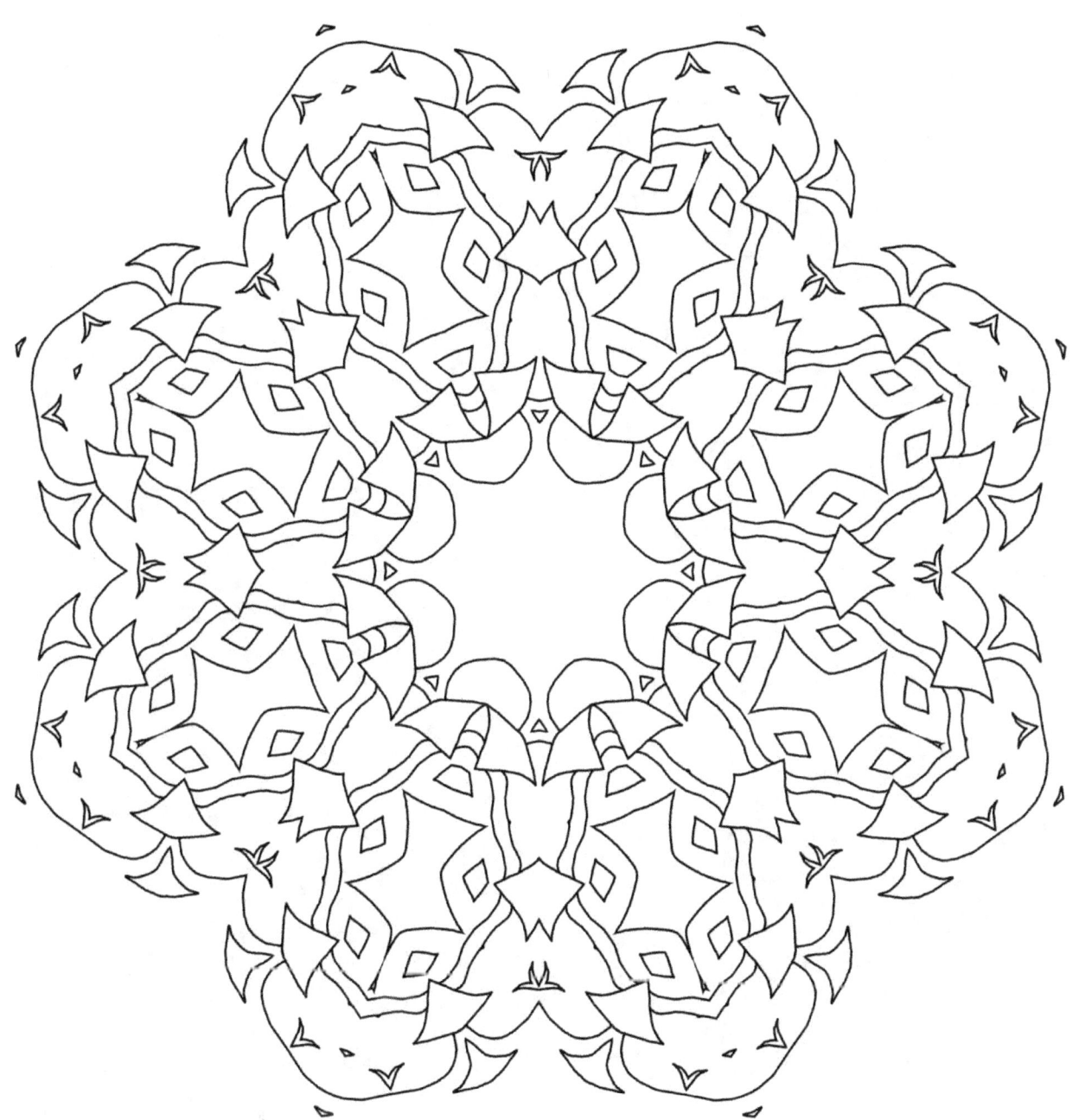

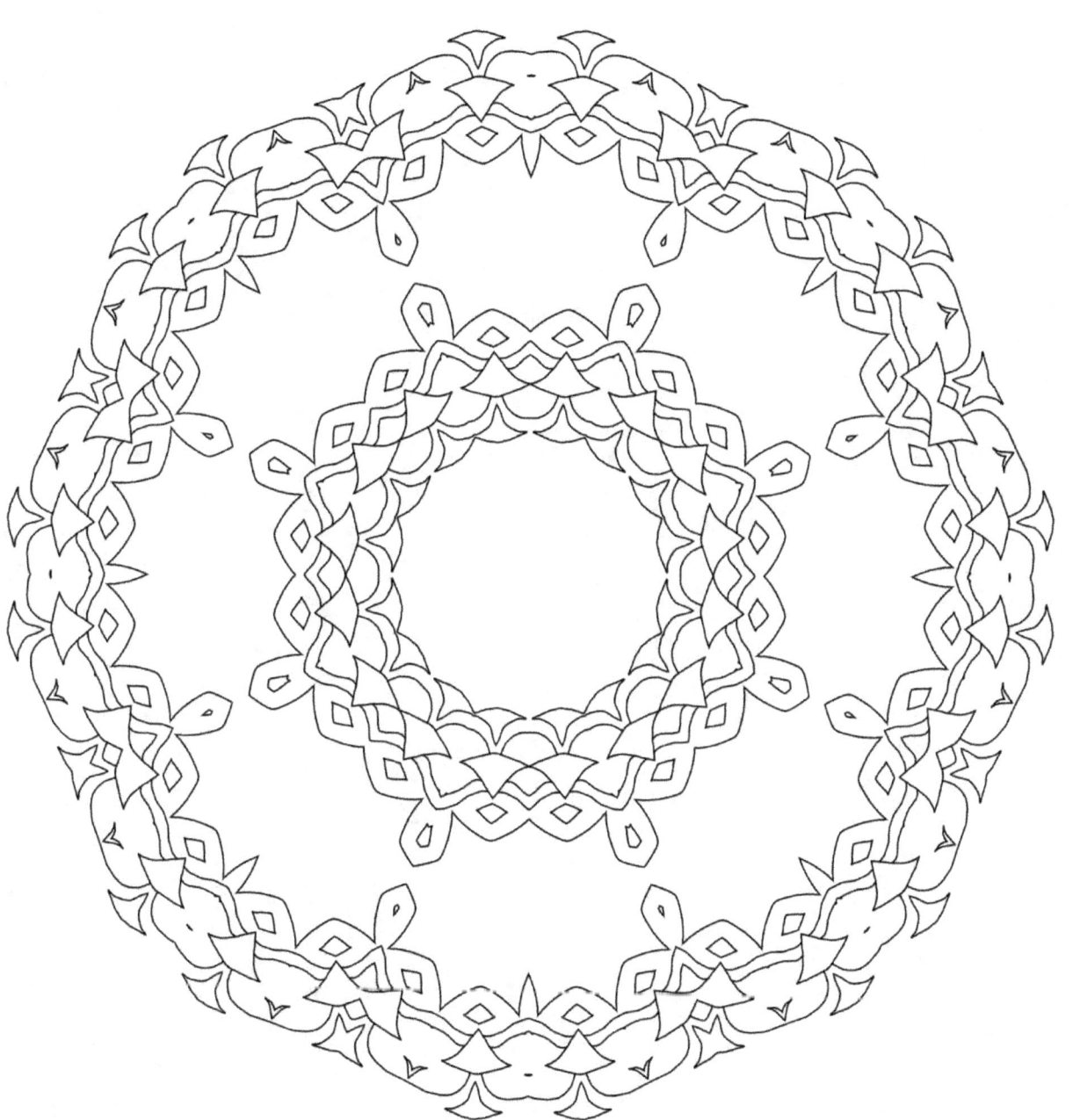

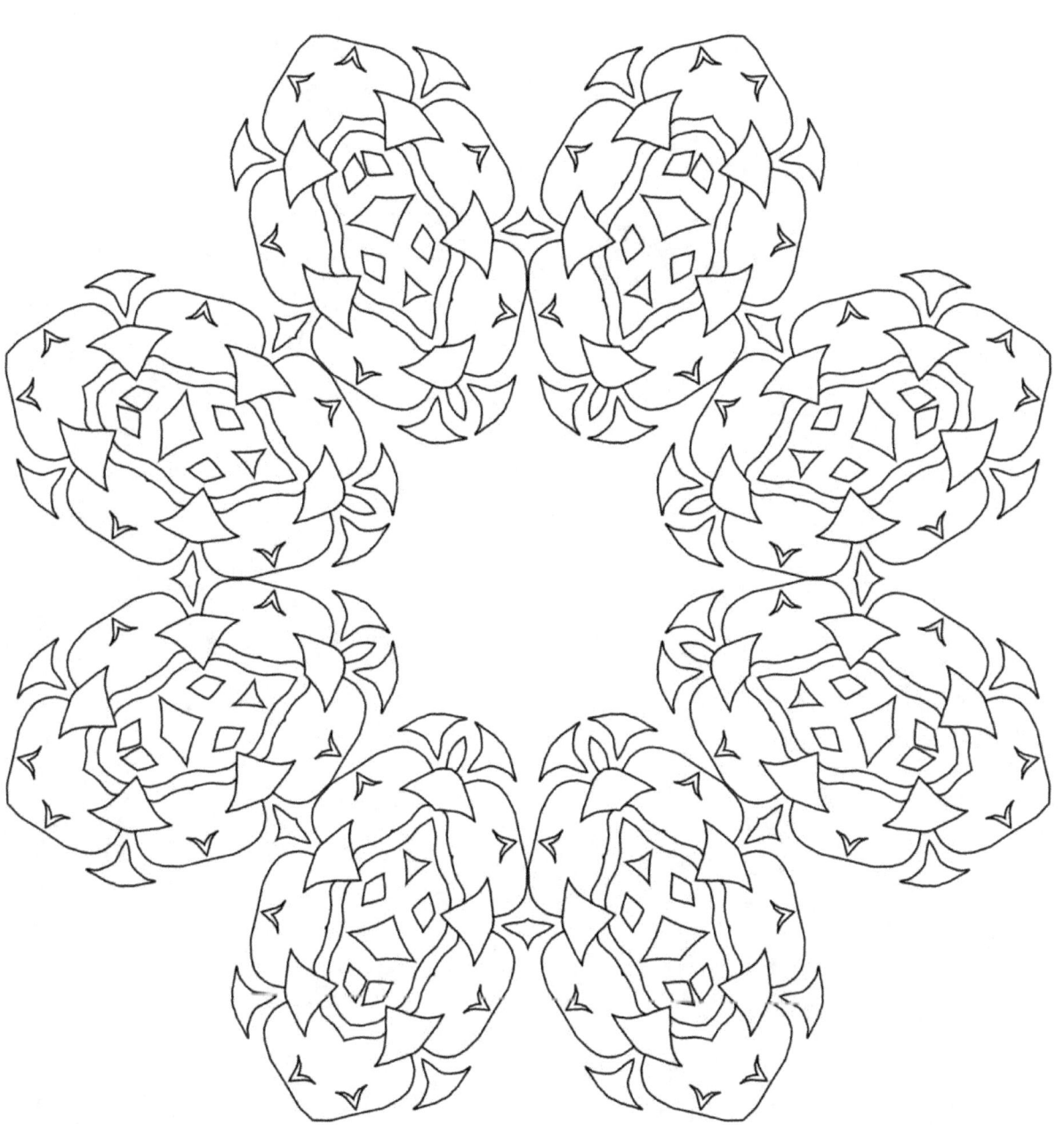

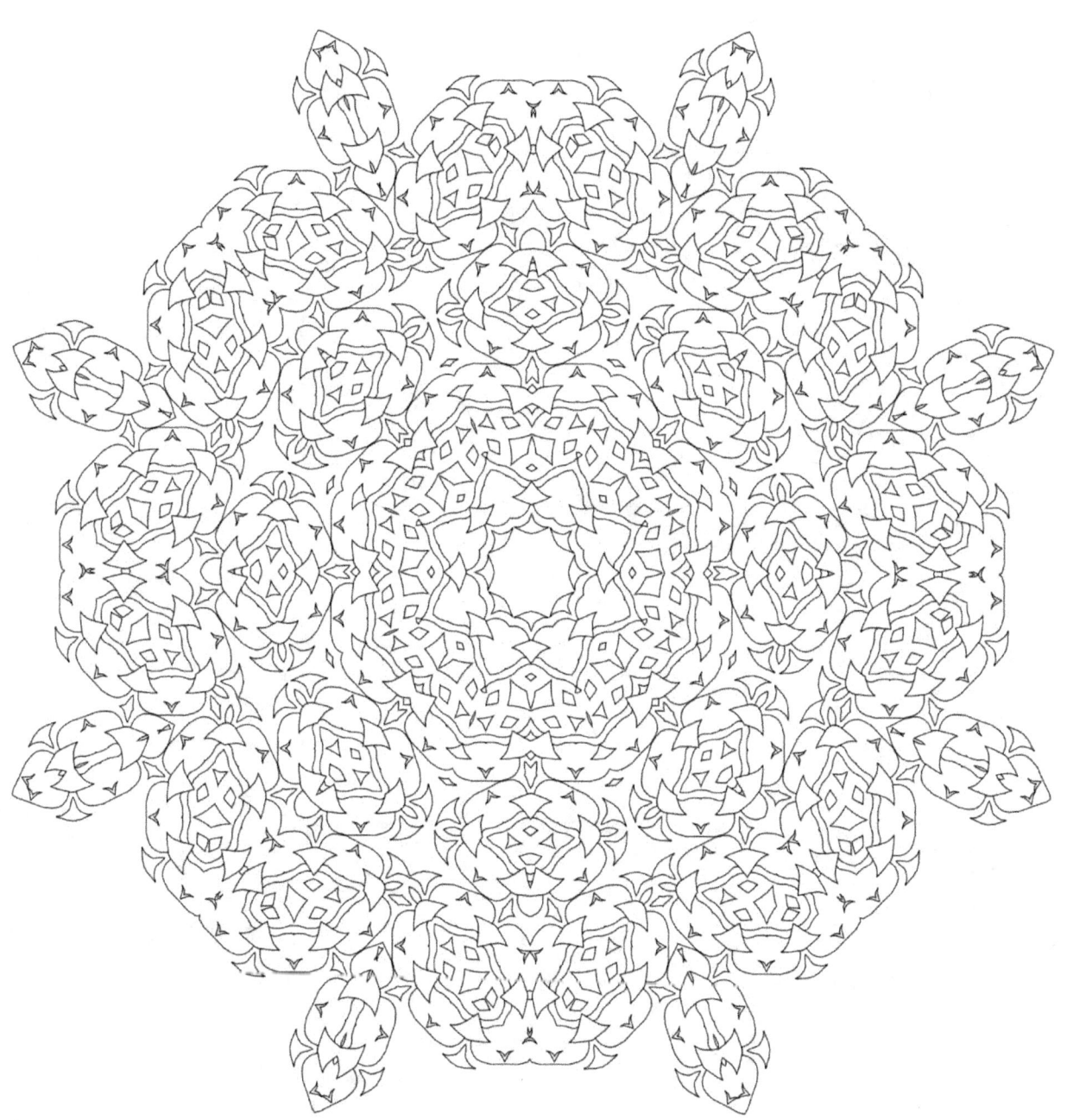

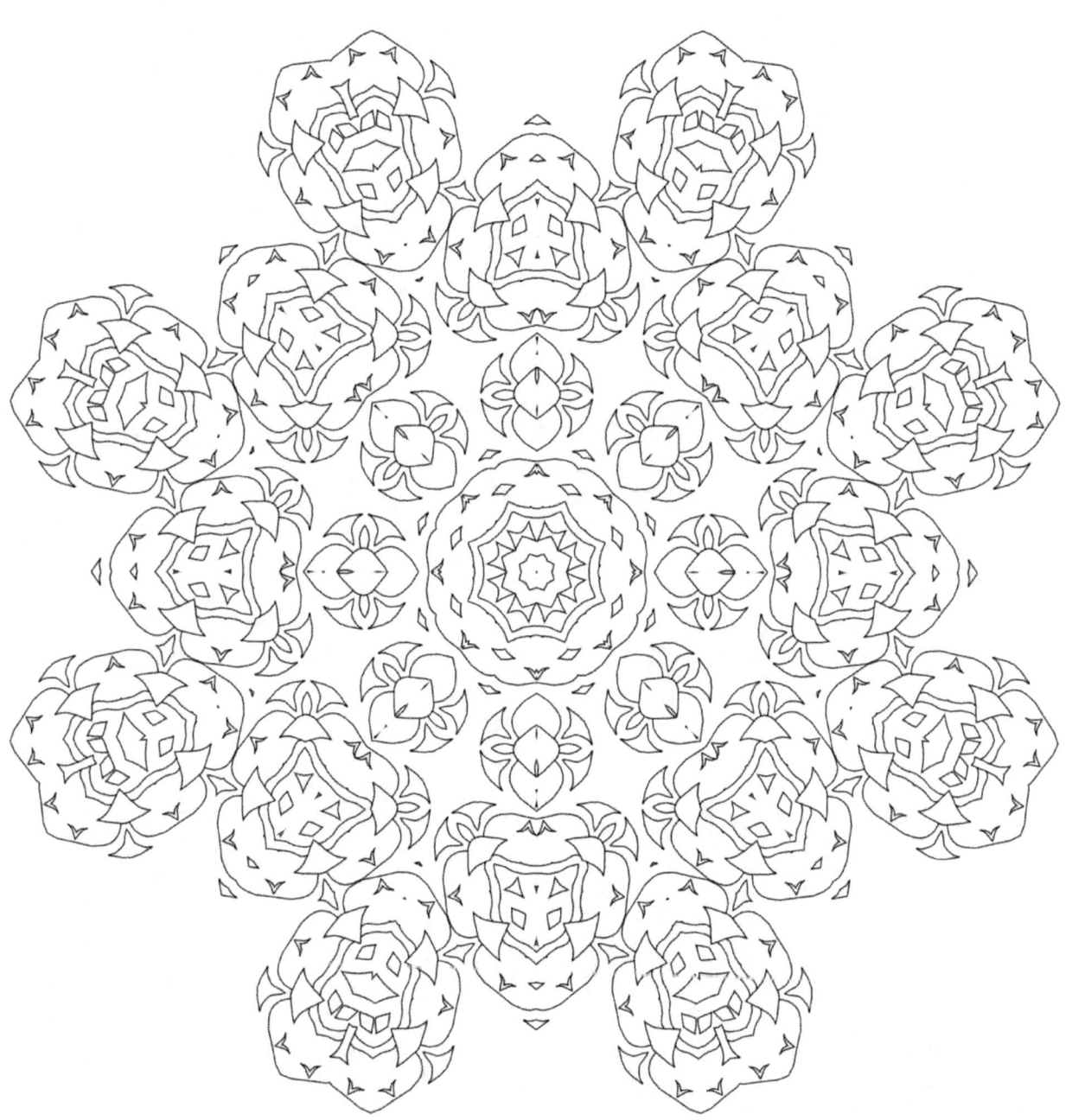

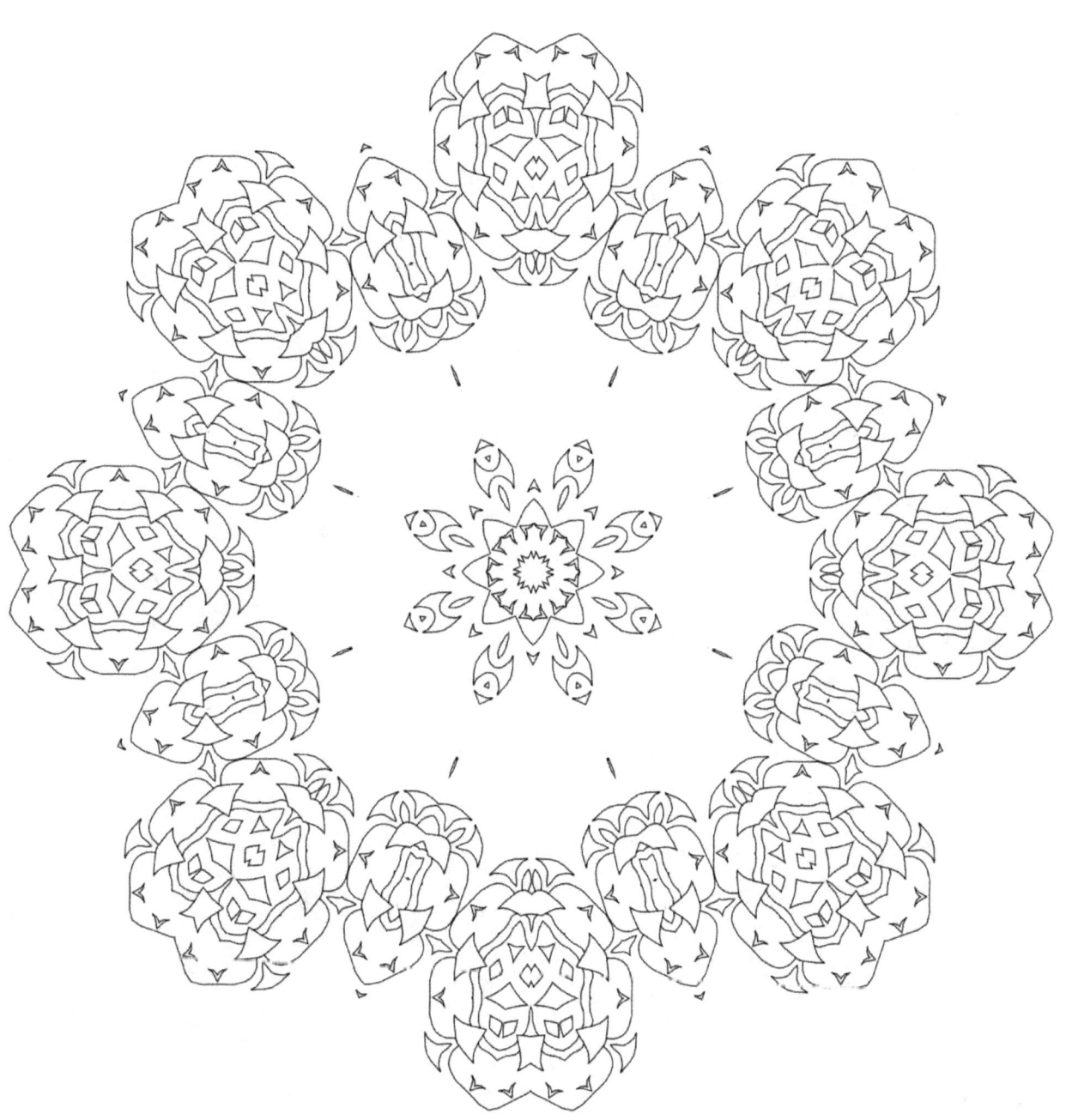

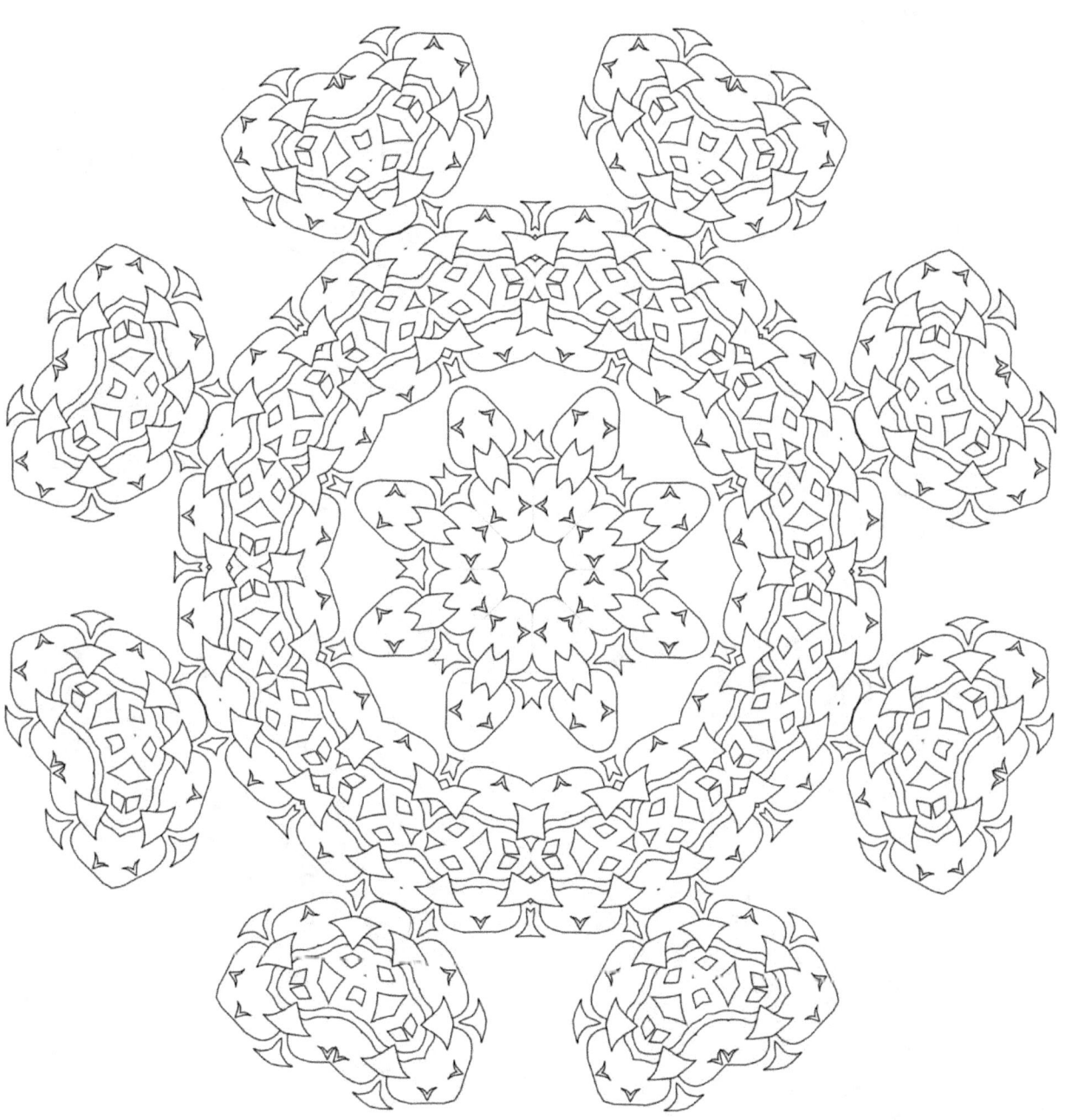

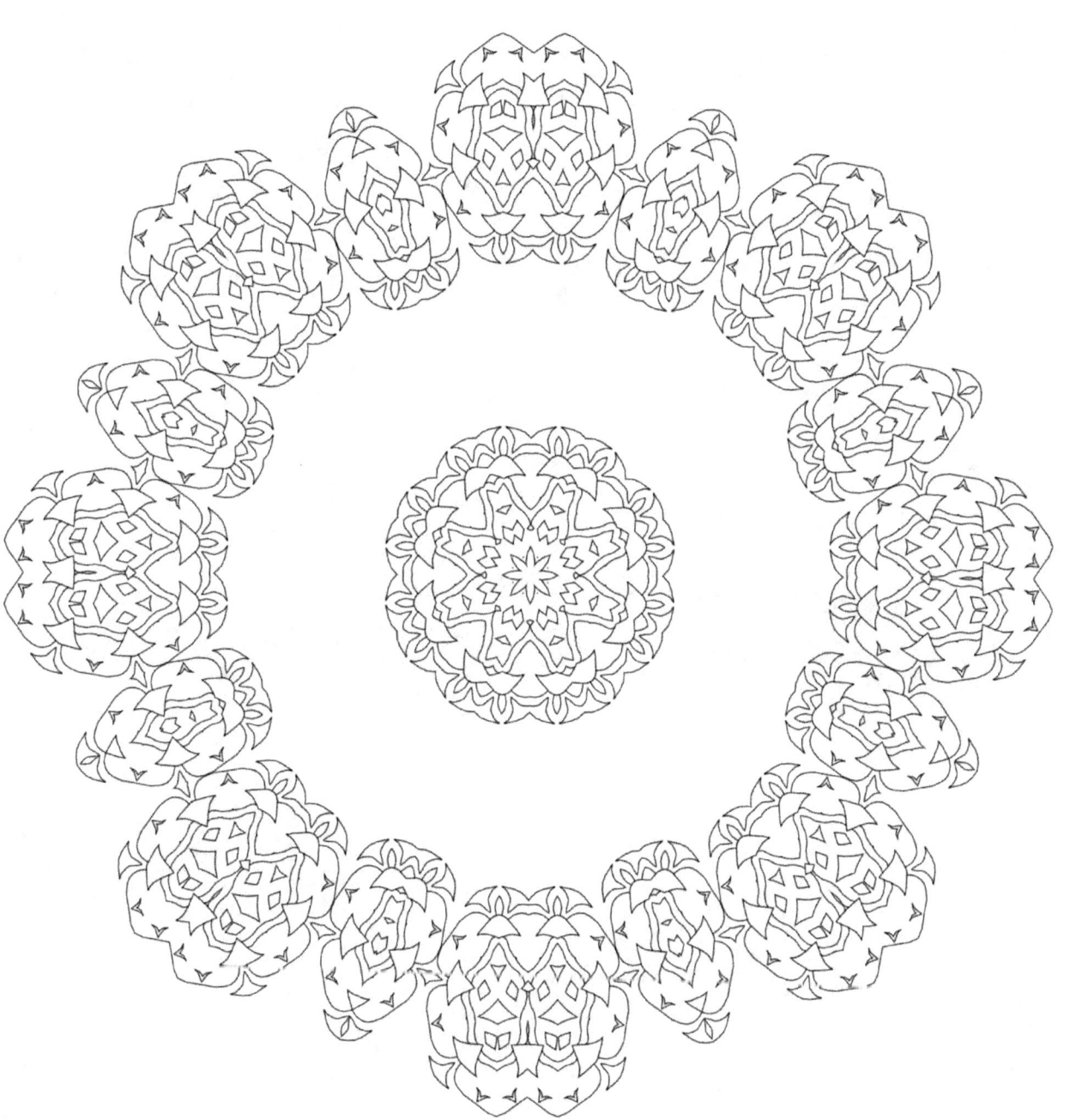

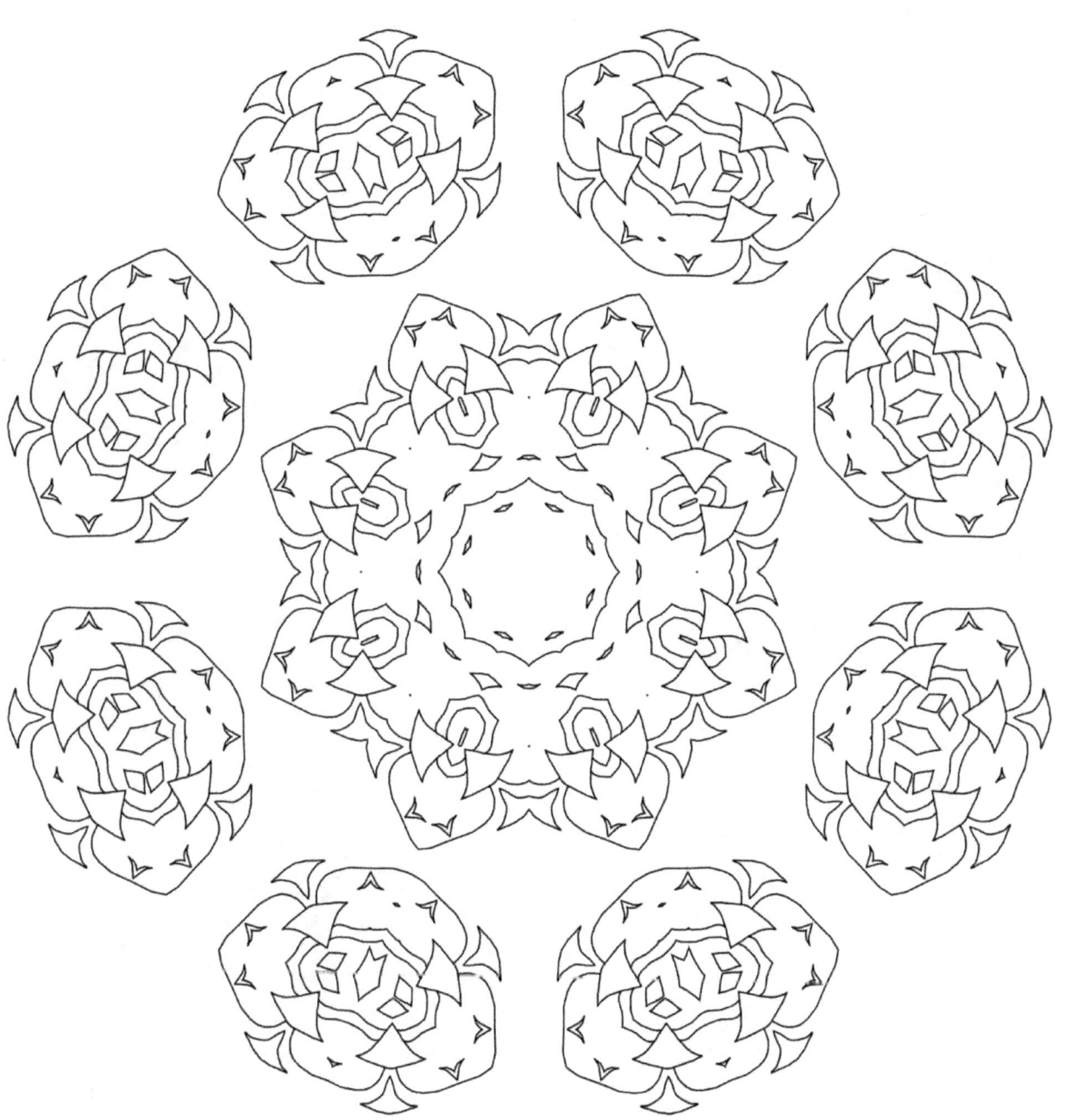

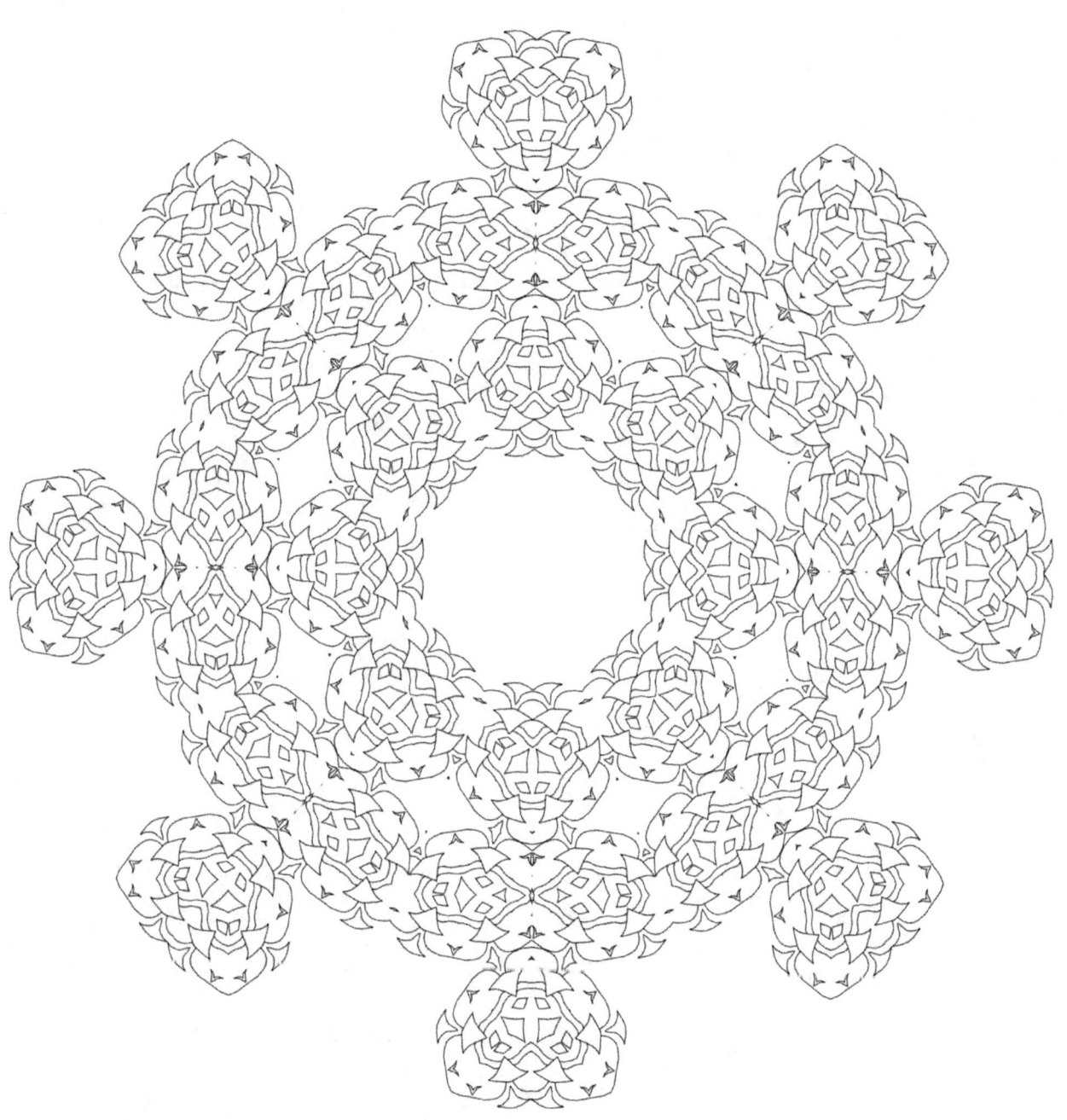

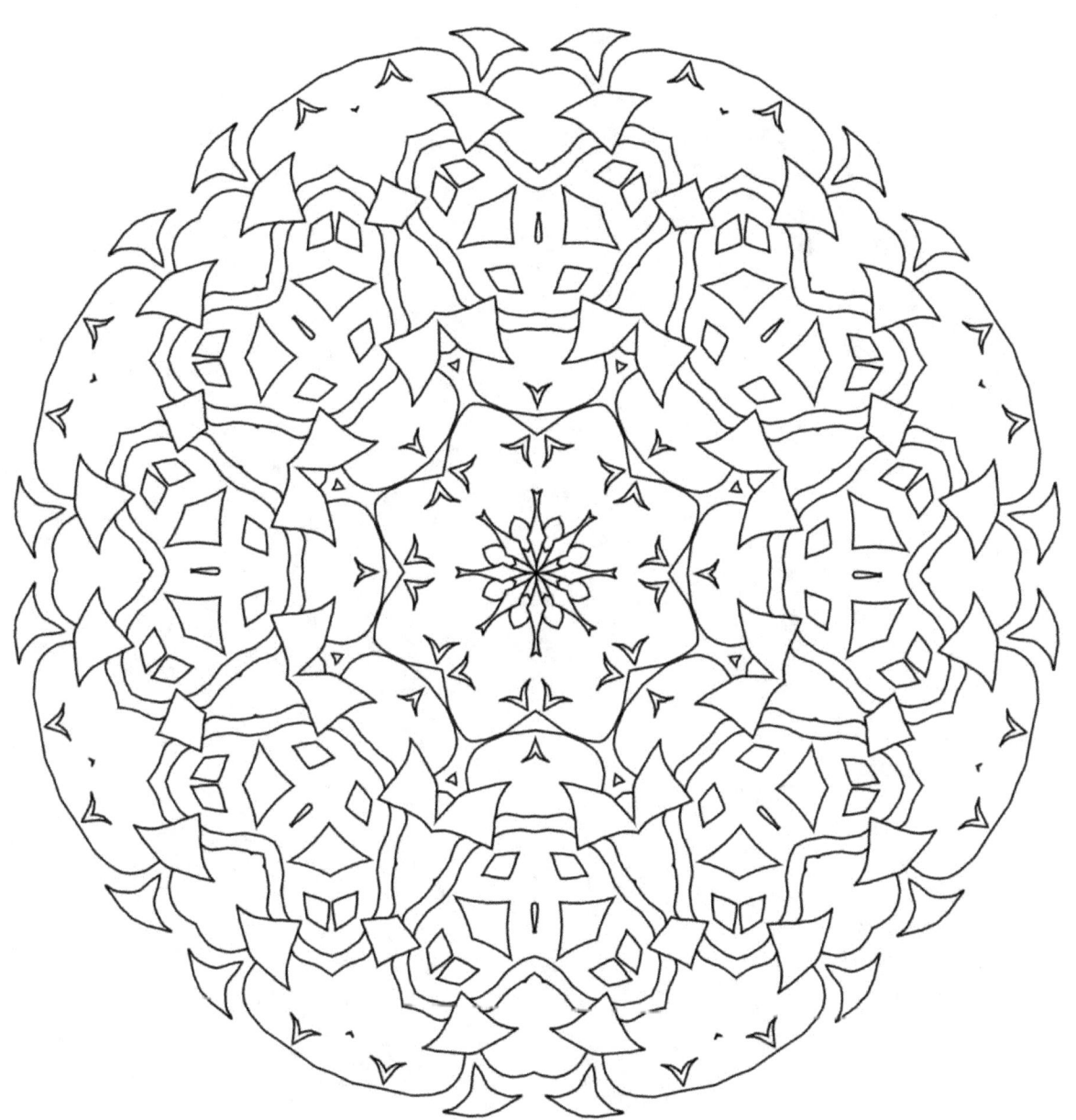

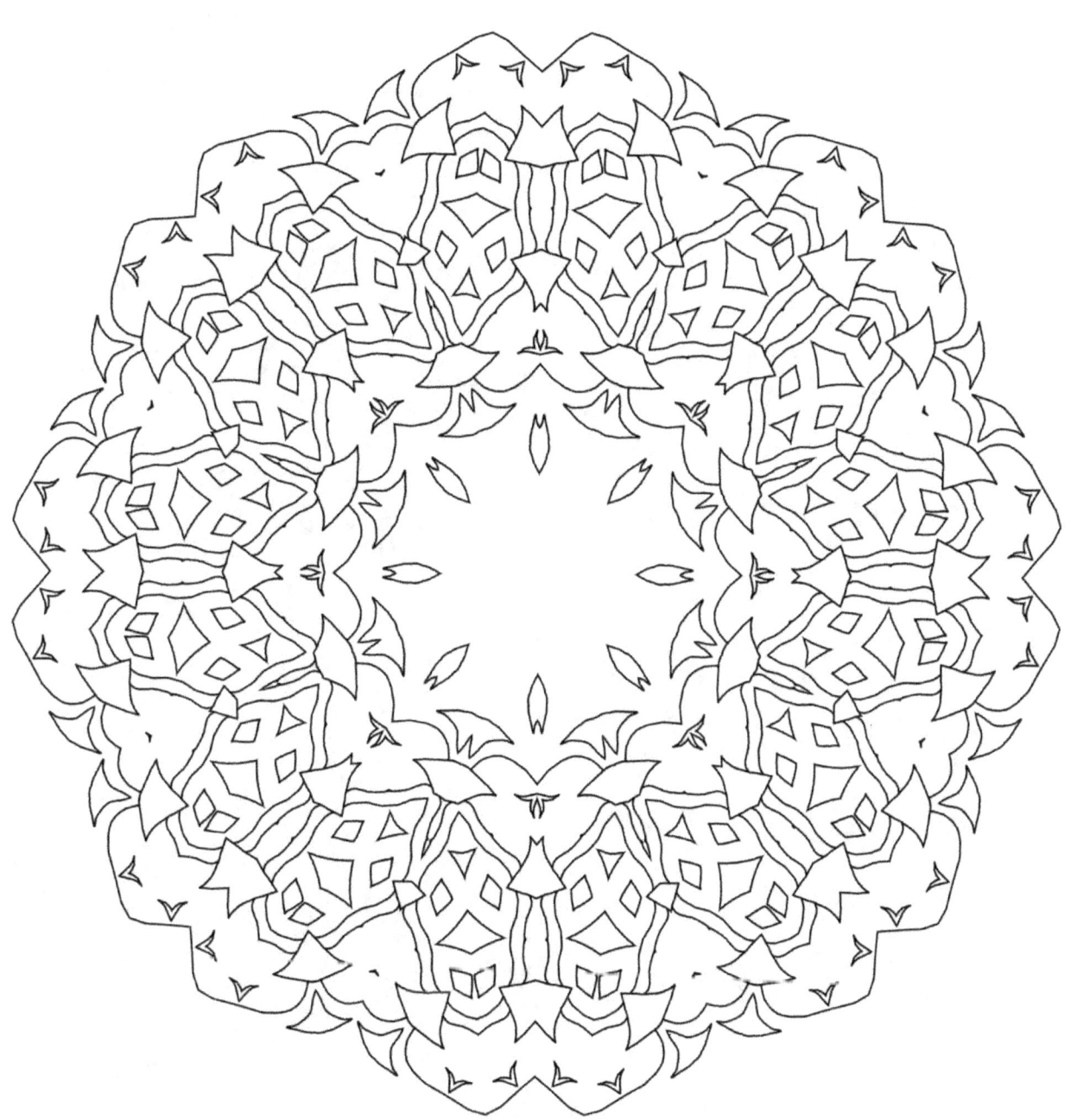

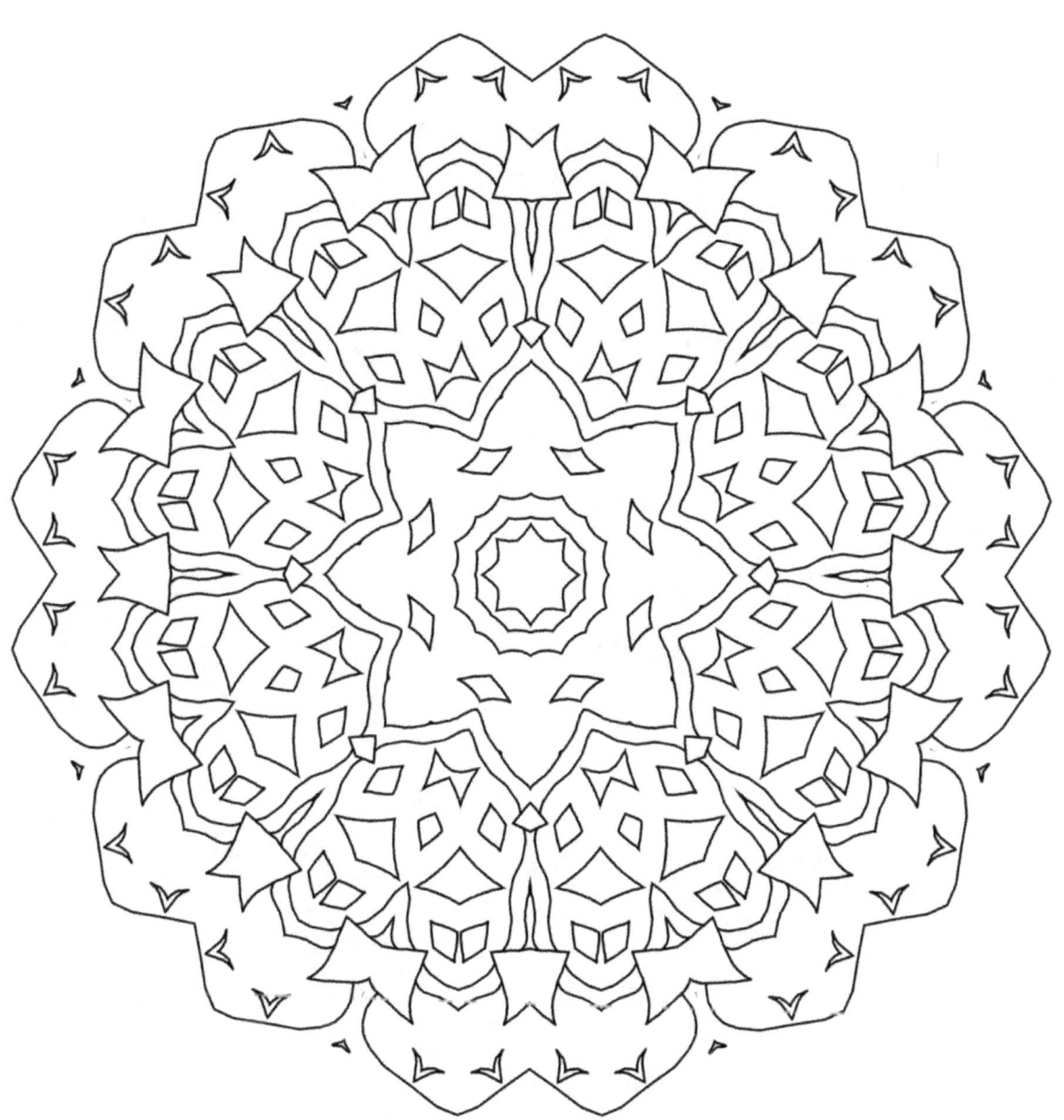

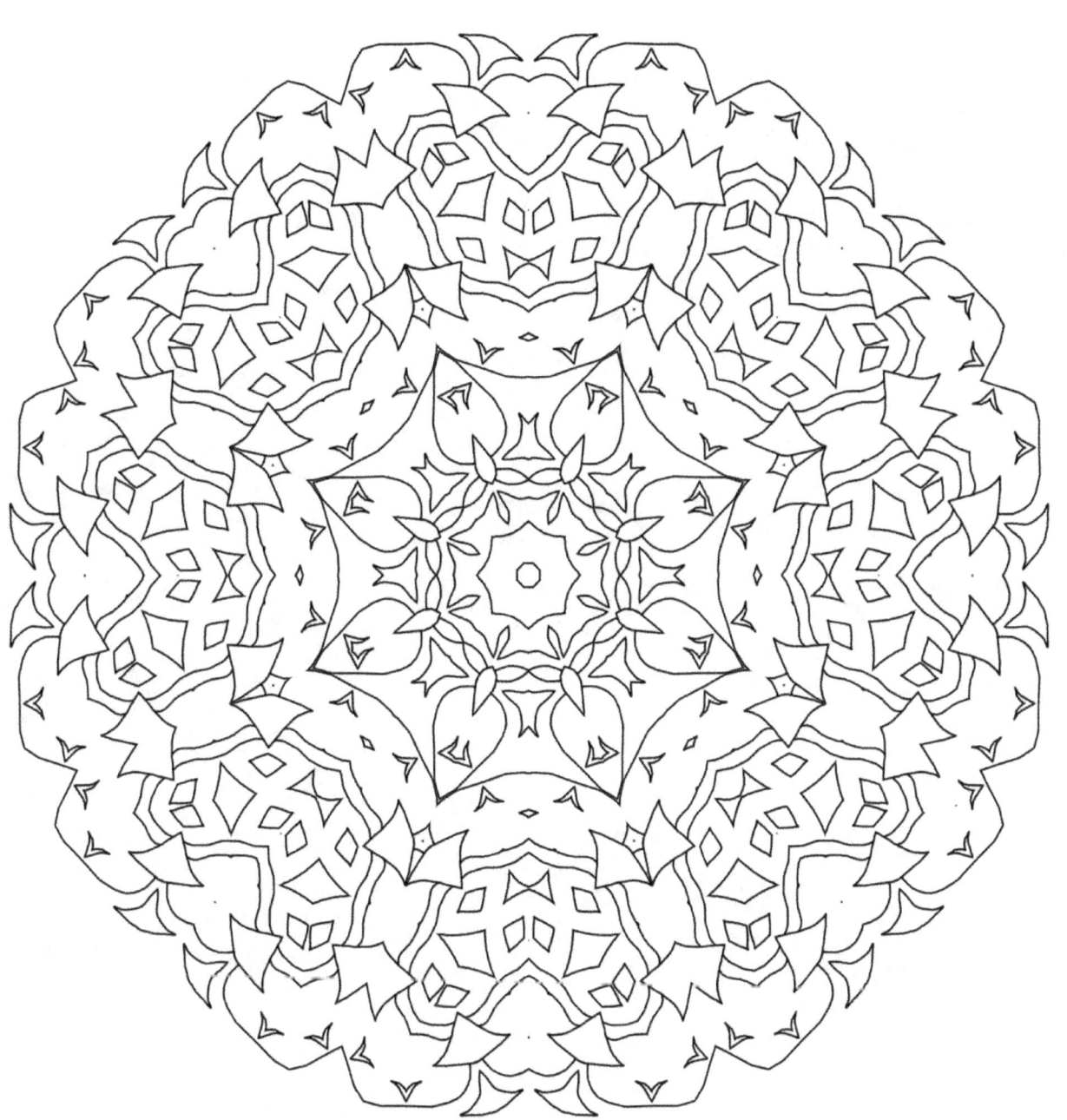

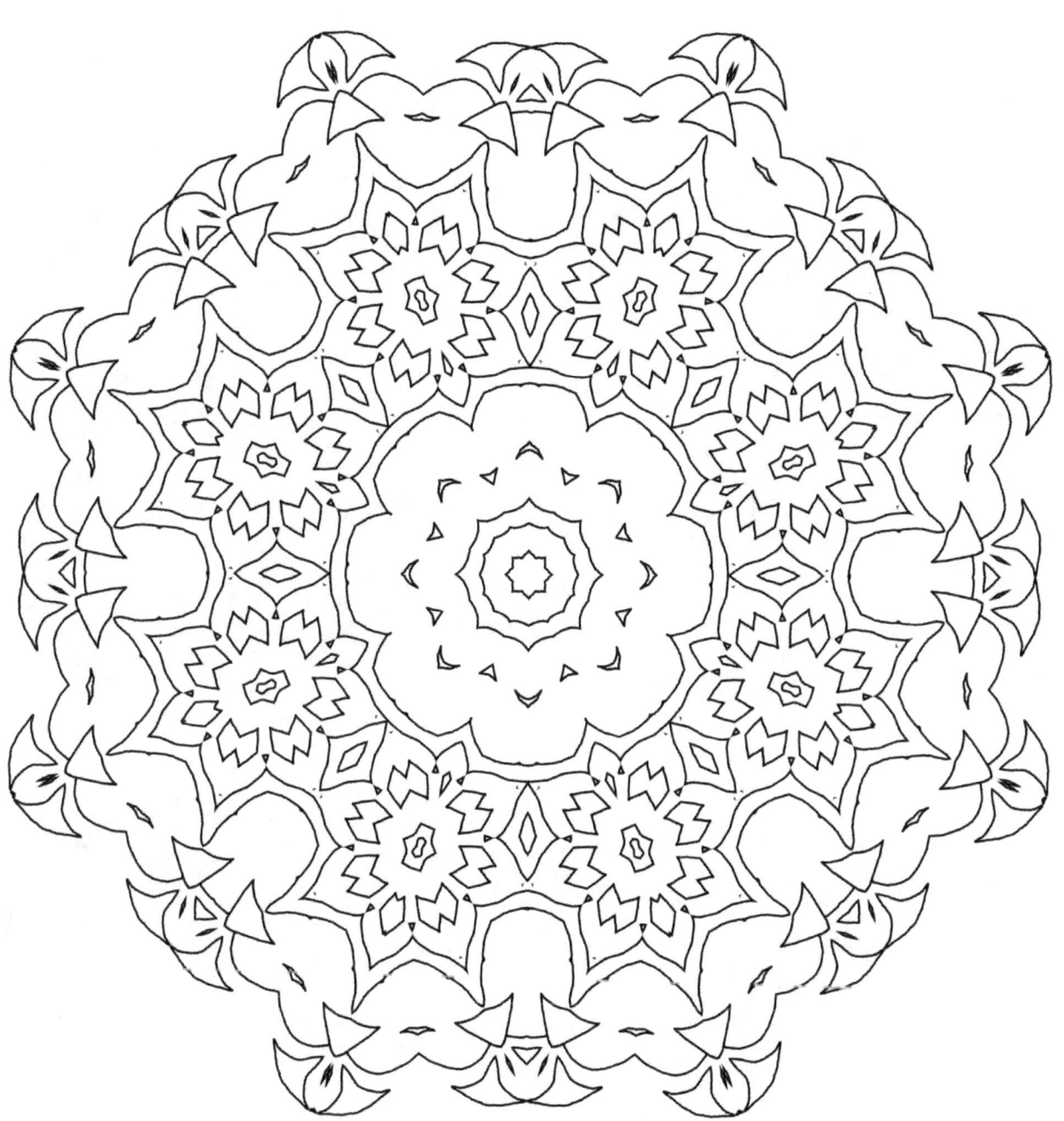

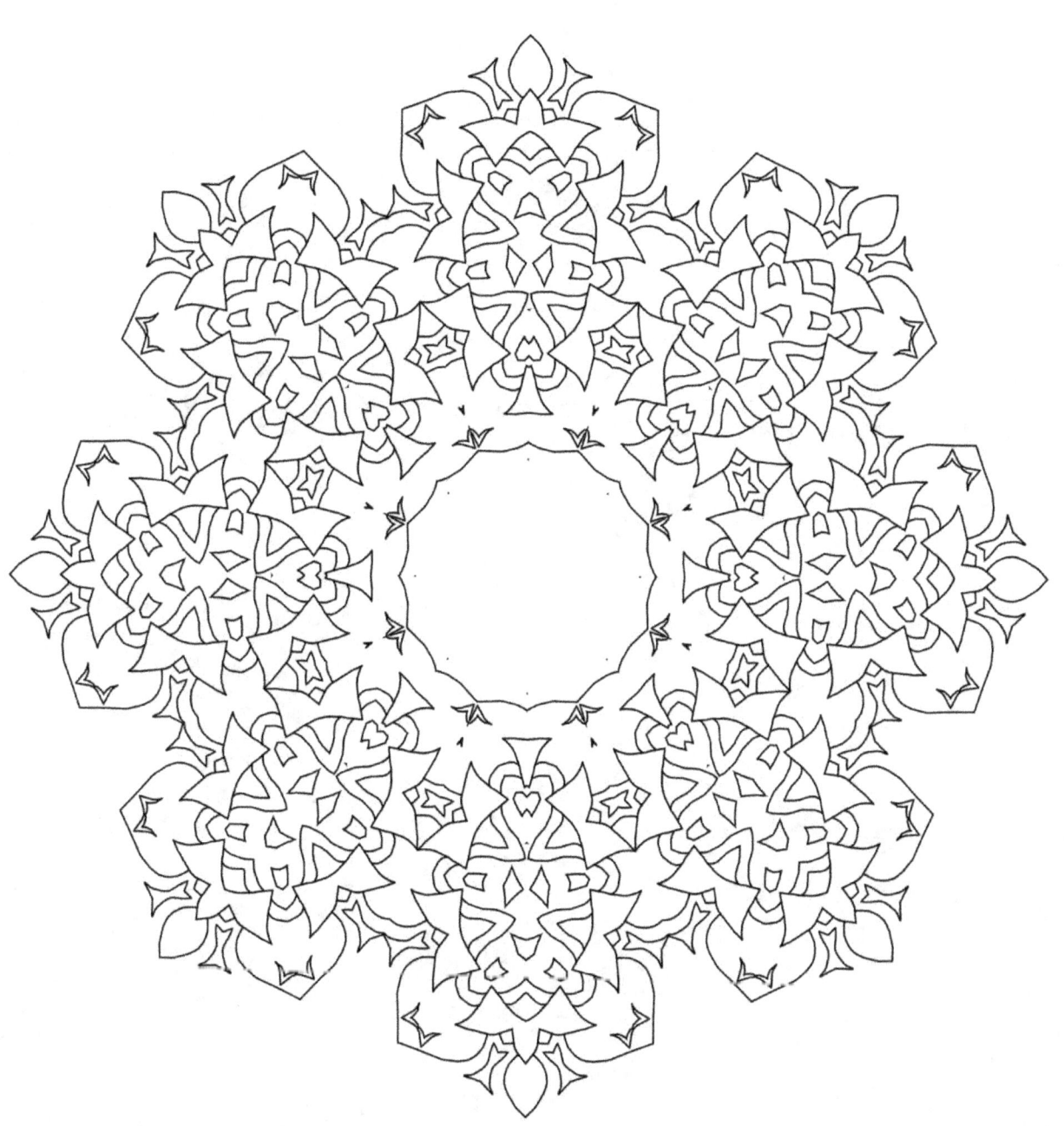

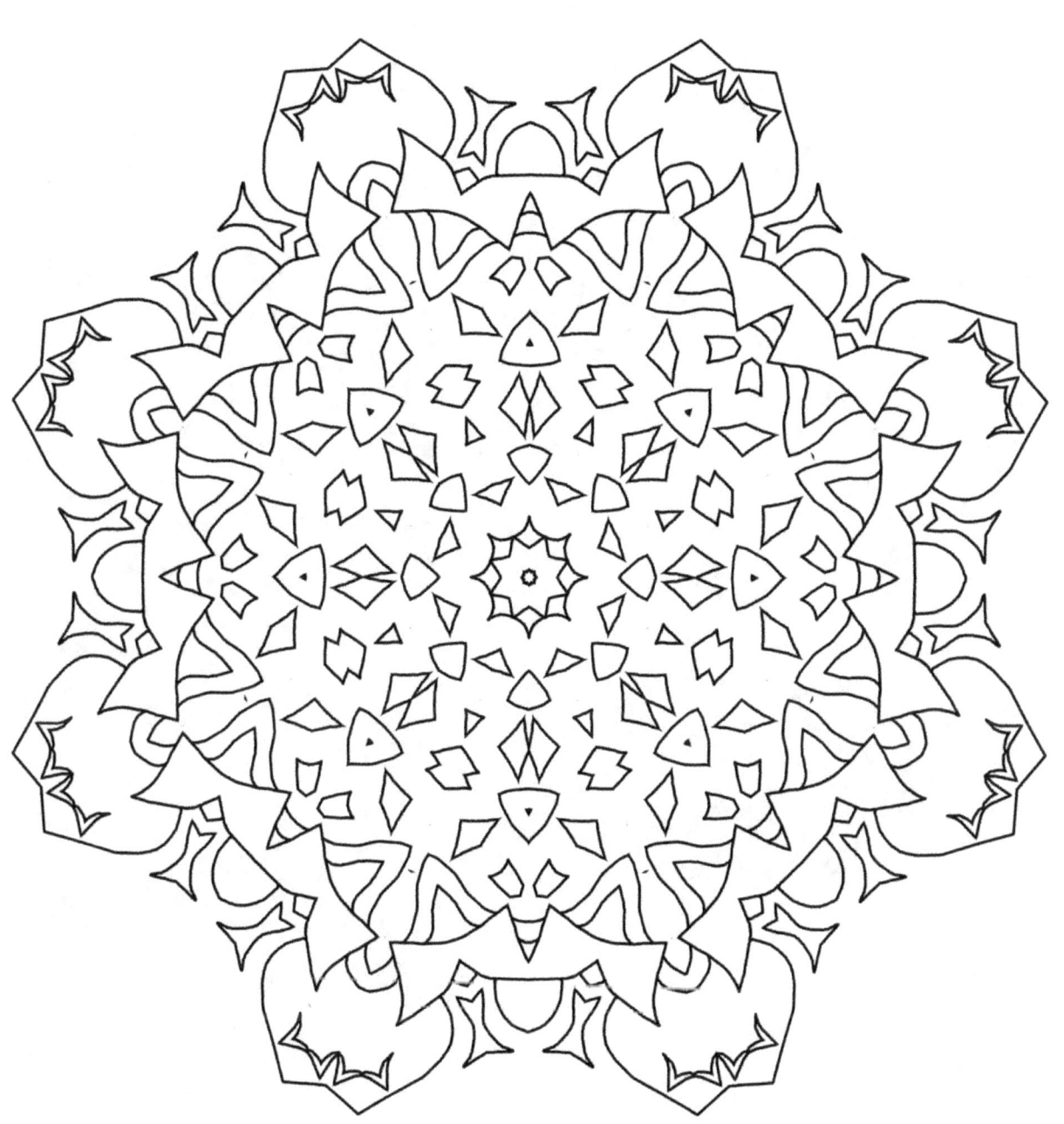

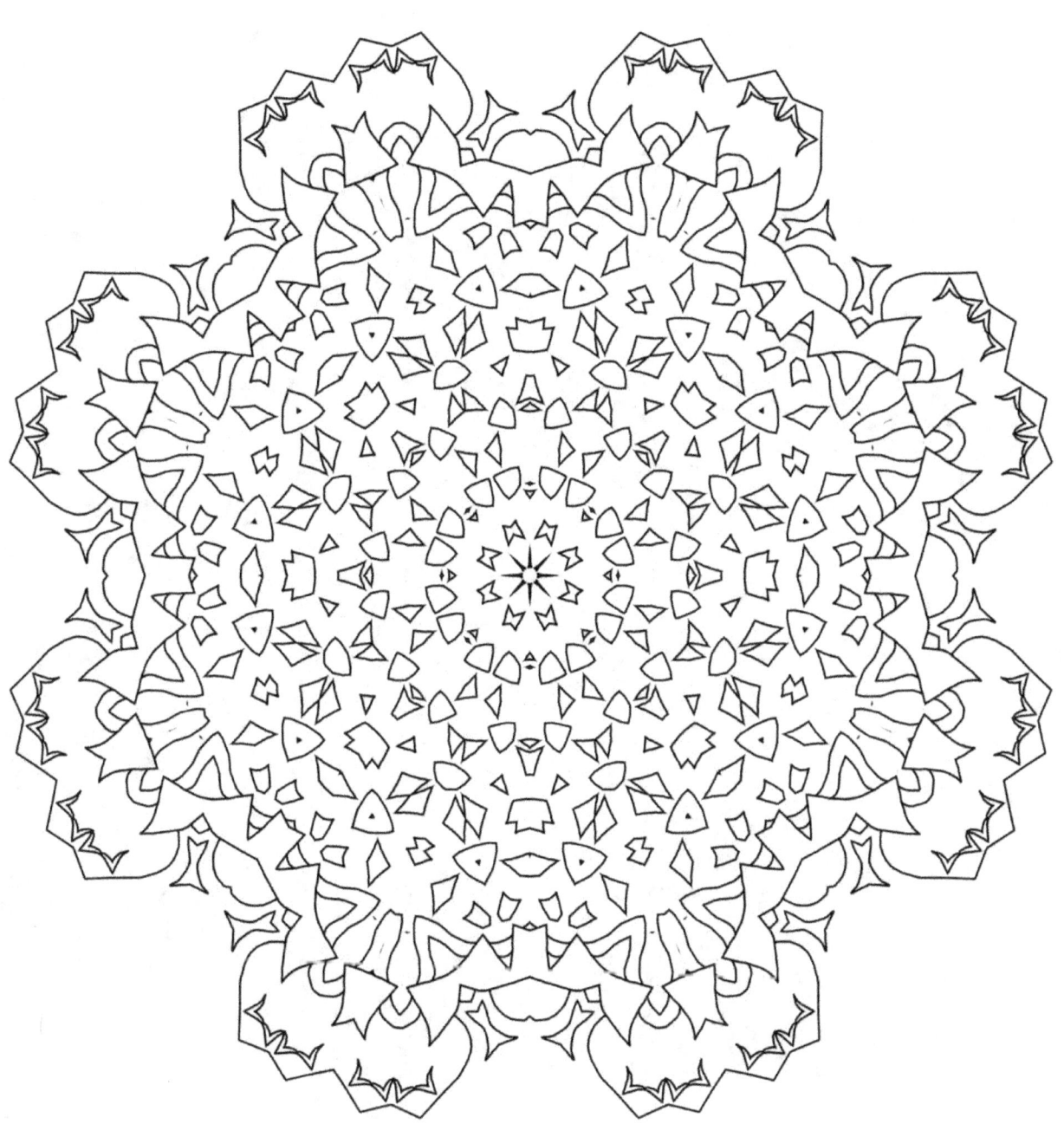

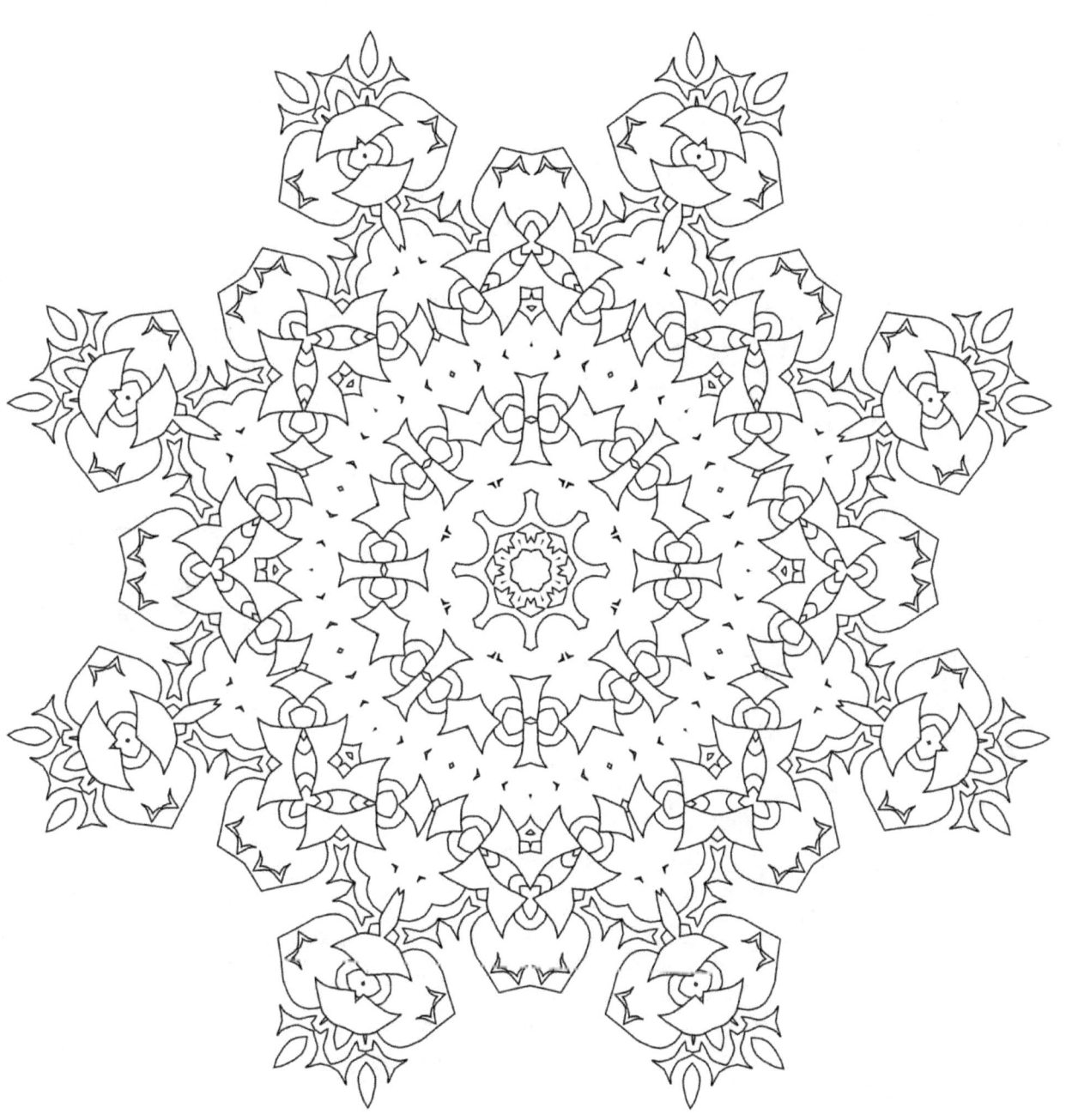

Thank you

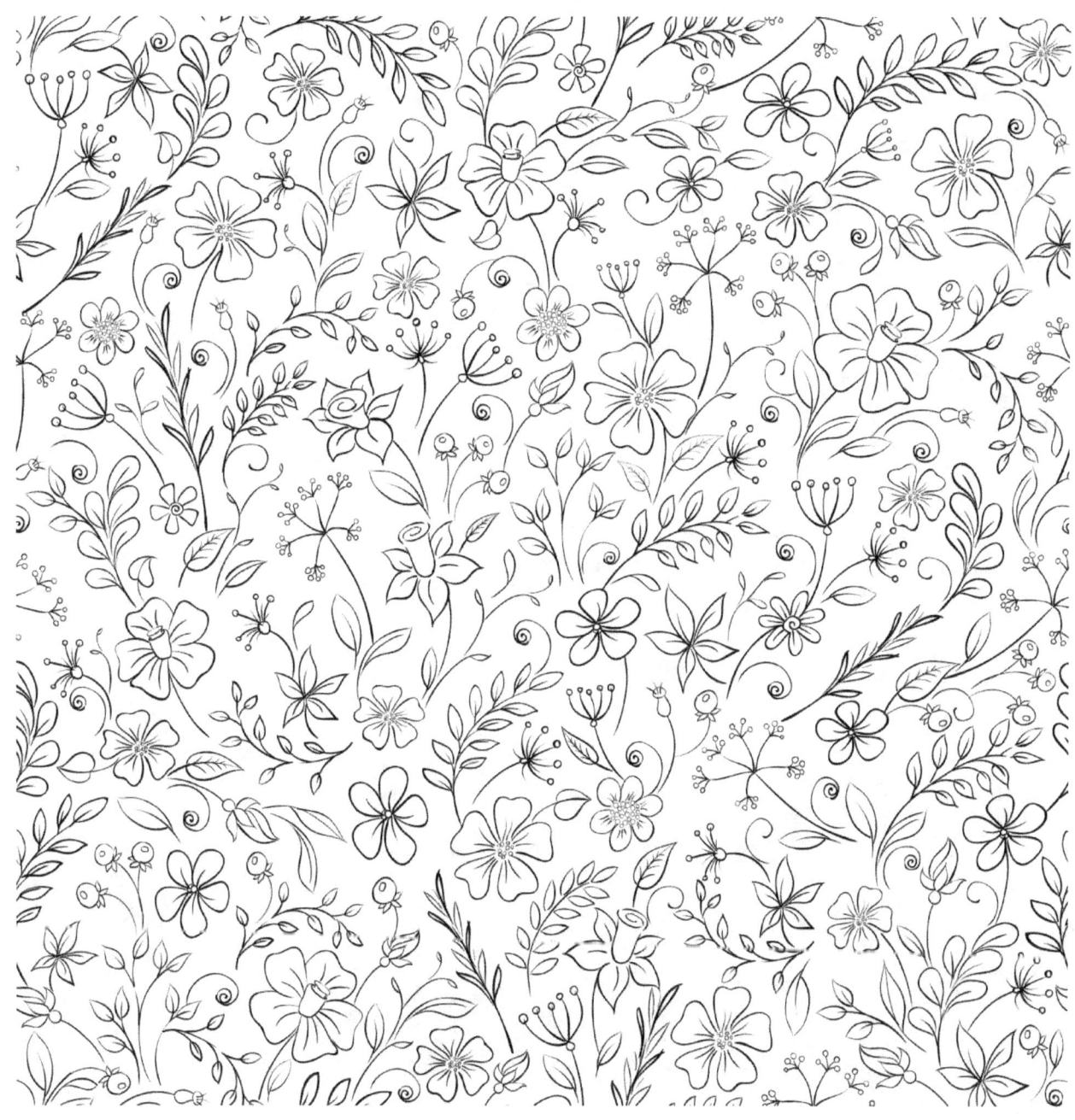

www.ingramcontent.com/pod-product-compliance
Lightning Source LLC
Chambersburg PA
CBHW081117180526
45170CB00008B/2877